[H.A.S.C. No. 114–98]

FULL SPECTRUM SECURITY CHALLENGES IN EUROPE AND THEIR EFFECTS ON DETERRENCE AND DEFENSE

_____

COMMITTEE ON ARMED SERVICES
HOUSE OF REPRESENTATIVES

ONE HUNDRED FOURTEENTH CONGRESS

SECOND SESSION

_____

HEARING HELD
FEBRUARY 25, 2016

_____

U.S. GOVERNMENT PUBLISHING OFFICE

99–629   WASHINGTON : 2017

For sale by the Superintendent of Documents, U.S. Government Publishing Office
Internet: bookstore.gpo.gov   Phone: toll free (866) 512–1800; DC area (202) 512–1800
Fax: (202) 512–2104   Mail: Stop IDCC, Washington, DC 20402–0001

COMMITTEE ON ARMED SERVICES

ONE HUNDRED FOURTEENTH CONGRESS

WILLIAM M. "MAC" THORNBERRY, Texas, *Chairman*

WALTER B. JONES, North Carolina
J. RANDY FORBES, Virginia
JEFF MILLER, Florida
JOE WILSON, South Carolina
FRANK A. LoBIONDO, New Jersey
ROB BISHOP, Utah
MICHAEL R. TURNER, Ohio
JOHN KLINE, Minnesota
MIKE ROGERS, Alabama
TRENT FRANKS, Arizona
BILL SHUSTER, Pennsylvania
K. MICHAEL CONAWAY, Texas
DOUG LAMBORN, Colorado
ROBERT J. WITTMAN, Virginia
DUNCAN HUNTER, California
JOHN FLEMING, Louisiana
MIKE COFFMAN, Colorado
CHRISTOPHER P. GIBSON, New York
VICKY HARTZLER, Missouri
JOSEPH J. HECK, Nevada
AUSTIN SCOTT, Georgia
MO BROOKS, Alabama
RICHARD B. NUGENT, Florida
PAUL COOK, California
JIM BRIDENSTINE, Oklahoma
BRAD R. WENSTRUP, Ohio
JACKIE WALORSKI, Indiana
BRADLEY BYRNE, Alabama
SAM GRAVES, Missouri
RYAN K. ZINKE, Montana
ELISE M. STEFANIK, New York
MARTHA McSALLY, Arizona
STEPHEN KNIGHT, California
THOMAS MacARTHUR, New Jersey
STEVE RUSSELL, Oklahoma

ADAM SMITH, Washington
LORETTA SANCHEZ, California
ROBERT A. BRADY, Pennsylvania
SUSAN A. DAVIS, California
JAMES R. LANGEVIN, Rhode Island
RICK LARSEN, Washington
JIM COOPER, Tennessee
MADELEINE Z. BORDALLO, Guam
JOE COURTNEY, Connecticut
NIKI TSONGAS, Massachusetts
JOHN GARAMENDI, California
HENRY C. "HANK" JOHNSON, JR., Georgia
JACKIE SPEIER, California
JOAQUIN CASTRO, Texas
TAMMY DUCKWORTH, Illinois
SCOTT H. PETERS, California
MARC A. VEASEY, Texas
TULSI GABBARD, Hawaii
TIMOTHY J. WALZ, Minnesota
BETO O'ROURKE, Texas
DONALD NORCROSS, New Jersey
RUBEN GALLEGO, Arizona
MARK TAKAI, Hawaii
GWEN GRAHAM, Florida
BRAD ASHFORD, Nebraska
SETH MOULTON, Massachusetts
PETE AGUILAR, California

ROBERT L. SIMMONS II, *Staff Director*
KATIE SENDAK, *Professional Staff Member*
WILLIAM S. JOHNSON, *Counsel*
BRITTON BURKETT, *Clerk*

(II)

CONTENTS

FULL SPECTRUM SECURITY CHALLENGES IN EUROPE AND THEIR EFFECTS ON DETERRENCE AND DEFENSE

House of Representatives,
Committee on Armed Services,
Washington, DC, Thursday, February 25, 2016.

The committee met, pursuant to call, at 10:03 a.m., in room 2118, Rayburn House Office Building, Hon. William M. "Mac" Thornberry (chairman of the committee) presiding.

OPENING STATEMENT OF HON. WILLIAM M. "MAC" THORN-BERRY, A REPRESENTATIVE FROM TEXAS, CHAIRMAN, COMMITTEE ON ARMED SERVICES

The CHAIRMAN. Committee will come to order. Seventy years ago next week, Winston Churchill gave his famous Iron Curtain speech in Fulton, Missouri. Among his insights was this, quote: "I do not believe that Soviet Russia desires war. What they desire is the fruits of war and the indefinite expansion of their power and doctrines."

He went on, "From what I have seen of our Russian friends and allies during the war I am convinced there is nothing they admire so much as strength and there is nothing for which they have less respect than weakness, especially military weakness," end quote.

I think what was true then is true now and we are seeing it play out before our eyes. The famous reset by the Obama administration with regard to Russia has not gone so well. Just over the past year or so Russia has consolidated its gains in Ukraine, has intervened in Syria, establishing a stronghold in the Middle East for the first time since the 1970s, and has continued to take unprecedented, provocative actions against NATO [North Atlantic Treaty Organization] ships and planes.

Russia presents a full spectrum of threats, from a modern nuclear arsenal which Putin has threatened to use against conventional forces, to hybrid tactics based on deception and confusion and little green men. So far, NATO and the U.S. have grappled to find effective countermeasures.

The President's budget proposal significantly—proposes to significantly increase our exercises in Eastern Europe as part of the European Reassurance Initiative. But rather than ask for more money to pay for it, his budget proposal would take it out of readiness, modernization—both of which have been under siege for years.

That can hardly leave the Russians quaking in their boots. Of course, Russia is not the only issue on the plate of our distinguished witness today. The growing threat of terrorist attack from ISIS [Islamic State in Iraq and Syria] coming both from Syria,

(1)

Iraq, and from Libya, as well as the migration of refugees more generally, are a significant issue for this theater.

In addition, whether a cyberattack would invoke Article 5 obligations under the NATO treaty, as we talked about in our hearing a couple weeks ago, is one of the many questions facing us all.

Finally, the security of Israel, which is also within this geographic command, is always a matter of keen interest and concern before this committee.

We are privileged to have before us a witness to help clarify all of these issues. Before introducing him I will turn to the gentlelady from California for any comments she would like to make.

STATEMENT OF HON. SUSAN A. DAVIS, A REPRESENTATIVE FROM CALIFORNIA, COMMITTEE ON ARMED SERVICES

Mrs. DAVIS. Thank you. Thank you, Mr. Chairman. I certainly ask unanimous consent that the ranking member's statement be entered into the record.

General——

The CHAIRMAN. Without objection.

[The prepared statement of Mr. Smith can be found in the Appendix on page 35.]

Mrs. DAVIS. General Breedlove, thank you very much for being here today with us, and as you conclude your time in command and you look to your retirement as well—and we hope that will be a good and smooth transition—I want to thank you for your work to enhance cooperation with our European partners and for moving us forward to address the challenges to Europe's security.

The chairman has made some excellent points, of course, about the complex and ever-changing situation that we face every day. I am very interested in your thoughts on Russian motivations and how U.S. and our allies can most effectively respond without pushing Russia—the Russian government to be even more adversarial.

Russia's destabilizing efforts continue, and it seems clear that Russian aggression and malign influence in Europe are likely the issues that the United States and our partners in Europe will have to grapple with for years to come. We must continue to lead in deterring Russian aggression and, if necessary, in concert with our partners—but our first priority has to be to prevent conflict.

I look forward to your testimony today and again thank you very much.

I yield back.

The CHAIRMAN. Our witness today is General Philip Breedlove, Supreme Allied Commander of our NATO forces and commander of the United States European Command.

General Breedlove, my understanding is that our current schedule is for you to rotate out of your current position and move on to other challenges after just about 40 years in the United States military. And so as we begin I want to thank you very much for your service in this position.

And throughout your career your interaction with this committee has been extremely valuable. You have been in a key position at a very critical time when literally the world has changed. And I know I speak on behalf of all our colleagues in thanking you for the way you have done this job especially, but also your entire military career.

Without objection, your entire witness statement will be made part of the record and we will turn the floor over to you.

STATEMENT OF GEN PHILIP M. BREEDLOVE, USAF, COMMANDER, UNITED STATES EUROPEAN COMMAND

General BREEDLOVE. Thank you, Mr. Chairman and Congresswoman Davis, distinguished members of the committee. Thank you for the opportunity to testify before you today.

I have had no greater honor in my 39-plus-year career than to lead the soldiers, sailors, airmen, Marines, Coast Guard, and civilians of the U.S. European Command [EUCOM]. These remarkable men and women serve not only in the EUCOM theater, but also in harm's way across the globe.

I thank this committee for your continued support to them and to their families.

I am also honored to serve alongside the men and women in uniform of the nations of Europe. They are willing and capable. They play an essential role in helping protect our own vital interests.

The last time I addressed this committee the security situation in Europe was complex. Since then, the situation has only grown more serious and more complicated.

Today Europe faces security challenges from two directions. First, to the east Europe faces a resurgent, aggressive Russia. Russia has chosen to be an adversary and poses a long-term existential threat to the United States and to our European allies and partners.

Russia is eager to exert unquestioned influence over its neighboring states to create a buffer zone, and Russia is extending its course of influence yet further afield to try to reestablish a leading role on the world stage.

Russia does not want to challenge the agreed rules of the international order; it wants to rewrite them. Russia sees the United States and NATO as threats to its objectives and as constraints on its aspirations. So Russia seeks to fracture our unity and challenge our resolve.

Russia, Mr. Chairman, as you said, recognizes strength and sees weakness as opportunity. To that end, Russia applies all instruments of national power, including its military, to coerce, corrupt, and undermine targeted European countries.

Some call this unconventional warfare; some call it hybrid; I like to talk about it as sending in little gray men who use their diplomatic, economic, and informational tools, in addition to military pressure, to shape and influence nations without triggering a NATO Article 5 military response.

To the south, from the Levant through North Africa, Europe faces a complicated mix of mass migration spurred by state instability and state collapse, and masking the movement of criminals, terrorists, and foreign fighters.

Within this mix ISIL [Islamic State of Iraq and the Levant], or Daesh, as I call them, is spreading like a cancer, taking advantage of paths of least resistance, threatening European nations and our own with terrorist attacks. Its brutality is driving millions to flee from Syria and Iraq, creating an almost unprecedented humanitarian challenge.

Russia's entry into the fight in Syria has wildly exacerbated the problem, changing the dynamic in the air and on the ground. Despite public pronouncements to the contrary, Russia has done little to counter Daesh but a great deal to bolster the Assad regime and its allies. And together, Russia and the Assad regime are deliberately weaponizing migration from Syria in an attempt to overwhelm European structures and break European resolve.

All genuinely constructive efforts to end the war are welcome, but that is not yet what we are seeing.

EUCOM is standing firm to meet this array of challenges. To counter Russia, EUCOM, working with allies and partners, is deterring Russia now and preparing to fight and win if necessary.

That demonstrated preparedness to defeat is an essential part of our deterrent message. To counter Daesh, EUCOM is actively facilitating intelligence-sharing and encouraging strong civil-military relationships across ministries and across borders.

And to meet all real and potential challenges, EUCOM is a central part of U.S. leadership in the NATO alliance as the alliance continues its adaptation through the Warsaw Summit, including the readiness and responsiveness of the entire NATO force structure.

This year's budget request reflects our solemn commitment to the security of our allies and partners and to protecting our homeland forward. EUCOM does not yet have the personnel, equipment, and resources necessary to carry out this growing mission.

But the continuation of the European Reassurance Initiative, or ERI, would strongly support EUCOM's efforts to counter Russian aggression and other threats by closing gaps in our posture and resourcing. EUCOM has carefully planned and executed the ERI funds you have authorized over the past 2 years, even as our headquarters has shrunk to become one of the smallest.

This year's budget request would significantly increase ERI funding to $3.4 billion. That would let us deepen our investment in Europe along five key lines of effort: providing more rotational forces, increasing training with our allies and partners, increasing prepositioned warfighting equipment in theater, increasing the capacities of our allies and partners, and improving the requisite supporting infrastructure.

Together, the tools ERI would provide would send a clear and visible message to all audiences of our strong will and resolve. Our further efforts to assure, deter, and defend, supported by ERI, would complement those of the entire whole-of-government team.

EUCOM remains committed to a shared vision of Europe whole, free, at peace, and prosperous.

Mr. Chairman, as my military career draws to an end I want to thank you again for your unwavering support of the men and women of our Armed Forces. And at this time I want to thank you for the personal opportunity to command them. I look forward to your questions.

[The prepared statement of General Breedlove can be found in the Appendix on page 37.]

The CHAIRMAN. Thank you, sir.

We had a hearing a couple weeks ago talking about Russia. Among the witnesses, for example, was your predecessor. And the question was raised, is ERI to really deter Russia or is it to make our allies feel better? And maybe it will do one but not the—the latter but not the former.

What is your view of that?

General BREEDLOVE. So, sir, I would agree with parts of that but I would like to elaborate on some others. I would agree that ERI does both assure our allies and I believe ERI begins the movement or the changes we need to make to fully deter Russia. But it is a step along that path.

For the past two decades, as you know, Mr. Chairman, we have been in the position where we have been trying to make a partner out of Russia in Europe. And we have downsized our forces, downsized our headquarters, capabilities, et cetera, to become a community that was focused on engaging Russia as a partner and building partnership capacity in Europe.

And what we now have is clearly not a partner in Russia. And so we have to begin reshaping the European Command and the NATO force structure to be able now to confront someone that does not wish to share our norms and values in Europe.

And those 20 years of change will not be overcome in one or two steps. ERI is one of the steps along the way to reposition us, I think, in forces, in headquarters capability, in the way we deal with our allies, to get to where we need to be to deter.

The CHAIRMAN. Well, let me follow up with one other question for you, and it really goes to the heart of deterrence, what deters. There was an article that just came out in the Foreign Affairs magazine that raises a point that I have thought about, and let me just read you a couple of sentences and then get your reaction.

This is an article entitled "Eurasia's Coming Anarchy," by Robert Kaplan. He says, "In China and Russia it is domestic insecurity that is breeding belligerence. Whereas aggression driven by domestic strength often follows a methodical, well-developed strategy, one that can be interpreted by other states which can then react appropriately, that fueled by domestic crisis results in daring, reactive, impulsive behavior which is much harder to forecast or counter."

And then he goes on to say, "Part of what Putin is doing is for the more chaos he can generate abroad, the more valuable the autocratic stability he provides at home will appear."

So I guess my interpretation of that is part of what is going on, especially in Russia and maybe China, is for domestic political concerns they gotta have outward aggression, and the last point was the more chaos out there the more valuable he tries—he believes it makes him for his internal purposes to stay in power.

But that makes it harder to deter, because if it is all about what is happening inside Russia then maybe this deterrence and ERI and other things isn't really going to get much done. I would appreciate your reaction to the thought and anything you can shed on that.

General BREEDLOVE. Thank you, Chairman. And I, again, would like to agree with some of the terms but elaborate on others.

You have heard me say before that deterrence is in the mind of the deterred. And so we are after the mind and the decision-making process of Mr. Putin.

And I did see some of the discussion you had with Jim Stavridis, and I would like to use a similar formulation in that what I believe Mr. Putin sees and will deter him is using all of the instruments of a nation's power—diplomatic, informational, military, and economic. But they are all required.

As you said in your opening statement and I did in mine, Mr. Putin understands strength and recognizes weakness. If we only use the diplomatic, the informational, and the economic to address Mr. Putin, he will see that the military is absent or, as I think Admiral Stavridis talked to you about, a lack of will to use the military may be absent.

And so I think that to deter Mr. Putin we have to have an all-of-government response which shows resistance diplomatically, informationally, militarily, and economically. And then, important to the military piece is not only having the capability and the capacity, but showing the will to use it if and when required.

Could I then address the other two pieces of your question?

First, exterior chaos: I believe exterior chaos is a tool that Mr. Putin likes to use to give him a platform to show that the great power of Russia needs to intervene in a West that cannot bring order to the world, and it gives him that platform to try to talk about the game that great Russia, as an equal player on the stage, bringing order.

The second piece that you talked about, sir, is domestic crisis inside the nation. I believe Mr. Putin is using a crisis inside his nation. I do believe that his people are feeling the drop in the oil prices, the sanctions, and the other things affecting his government.

But he uses that to focus them on an external enemy to bring their focus to what he wants to do with his nation and his power. And he is now focusing his people completely on the United States first and foremost, and secondarily NATO as an external enemy that they need to be ready to rise up to meet.

The CHAIRMAN. Thank you.

Mrs. Davis.

Mrs. DAVIS. Thank you very much, General, for being here.

Thank you, Mr. Chairman.

We have an opportunity to work with our allies, our partners, and I think the discussion that you just had with the chairman is very helpful. Is that something that you feel is understood throughout the—our allied community?

General BREEDLOVE. Ma'am, I do. But understood is not attached always to the kind of action that maybe we would seek or hope for. But I will tell you that I am an optimist here. I am more of a glass full—half-full in the way our allies are now approaching the security environment in Europe.

In Wales we saw the leading edge of the problems in Ukraine and we made the biggest changes to NATO ever, and some things are going extremely well—most things are going extremely well in that change. The military things we have done to change at a very high level this joint task force, the way we have organized our headquarters, the overall changes in the readiness and responsiveness of NATO forces, most specifically the ERF [European Rotational Force]—all these things are completely moving apace to be completed before Warsaw, and we have deployed and demonstrated them.

And as I mentioned to you in not the too-distant past, we see the nations now turning around budgets. The numbers may be wrong; it changes from day to day. But 16 to 17 of our nations have stopped declines in their budgets; 5 were over 2 percent; 6 or 7 now have a credible plan to get to 2 percent spending in a reasonable amount of time.

So I have seen change which is good.

Mrs. DAVIS. And the European Reassurance Initiative—how do you see that as a tool then for us to support, I think, those efforts specifically? And I just want to get a sense of—you mentioned that this is not going to be a 1-year budget. As I understand it, this is part of our Overseas Contingency Operation funds, and yet it is something that is going to have to continue.

What would that look like to you? We are sorry that you are going to be leaving the command, but we know that you want to leave something in place. What should that look like as we move forward?

General BREEDLOVE. So, ma'am, as I explained before, and I won't go too far back but we have got about 20 years of a different paradigm to correct. We are on our third—we will have had 2 years of ERI and we are now asking for this third year of ERI.

We have kept, as you heard me mention in my opening remarks, a focus on basically five areas.

Infrastructure—and that is not building buildings, that is fixing ports, fixing rail yards, changing exercise and training areas, changing storage areas in order to make it easier for us to rapidly reinforce Europe.

Preposition of equipment we talked about, and that is that we are in this ERI looking to bring across our second heavy force to put into preposition status. And this one will be used not for practicing but for warfighting.

We are using the ERI to rotationally increase our forward force structure. I have been very straightforward: There is no real substitute for permanently forward-stationed forces. But a second best, which is acceptable and which is where we are heading, is to have a heel-to-toe rotational forces fully funded to increase our presence in Europe, and that is a part of the ERI.

Building the partnership capacity, bringing other nations in the NATO alliance up alongside of us in the skill sets and capabilities we need.

And then the last piece: training and exercise with our partners.

So I don't mean to build a watch, but those five elements are going to be needed to be sustained for some number of years to get us to that position where we believe we are now in the position where we can deter—as well as ensure, but deter. And we are working now on what that future position we think should be.

Mrs. DAVIS. Thank you, sir. And I think as people are refining that further that will be helpful for us to know and to work with our budget folks, as well.

Thank you.

The CHAIRMAN. Mr. Turner.

Mr. TURNER. Thank you, Mr. Chairman.

I want to join with you in thanking General Breedlove for your service. It has been an incredibly important time for you to be in Europe because you have both been incredibly articulate of the rising threat of Russia but not alarmist. You have balanced in telling us policymakers and decision makers as to what we need to do to give you the tools to change the dynamics.

You and I have discussed the very public RAND study that most recently has tried to give a picture of that vulnerability, looking at the Baltics perhaps being available within 60 hours to Russia's new aggression, their modernization, and their forces.

I appreciate your use of the word "deter" because it is incredibly important that we deter aggression, not just meet aggression. Preventing it from happening in the first place is going to require a military force for which there would be risk to the other side.

You have indicated prepositioning as an important aspect. I would like to talk to you about two aspects of our change in posture that we need. And General Ben Hodges, who is the commanding general of U.S. Army Europe, has stated that, quote: "There used to be 300,000 soldiers in Europe during the height of the Cold War. Today we have 30,000 with the same mission: to assure allies and to deter Russia." There is a big difference between 300,000 and 30,000.

So there are two vulnerabilities that we have, in listening to your comments; and I would like to know how to address them.

One: We don't know what we used to know about what Russia is doing. We used to have all eyes on them and when they would do buildups and preparations for what you described as snap exercises we knew where they were going, what they were doing, and how they were going to do it.

And two: With the concept of prepositioning, you know, we just don't have what we need there and we might not be able to get there. In the RAND study they point out the vulnerability of playing an away game while the adversary is playing a home game.

Could you please describe what we need to be doing in both the aspects of greater understanding, greater visibility into Russia's actions and what they are doing, and secondly, then, emphasize again your statements of our need to have forces there?

General BREEDLOVE. Sir, thank you very much for the question, and I will try not to go long because it is quite a—to walk this from left to right will take a moment. First and foremost, a lot of smart people in RAND. I really love their work and I have known most of these people most of my military career.

But what you find from a study is tied a lot to how you have been given the problem. And what is the status of the forces at the beginning of a problem I think is at the heart of the matter of the question you are asking me.

We used to have a very persistent and capable look at Russia at the strategic level, the operational level, and the tactical level so that we could understand what they were doing with their forces. And we built a robust system of indications and warnings, INW, that was based on that robust intel.

For the past 20 years we have been refocusing—for all the right reasons, I think you would agree—some of our intelligence on Al Qaeda, Daesh, Taliban, other elements around the world. And so for the past 20 years, as we have been trying to make Russia a partner we have reapportioned a large portion of our ability to see away from Russia and towards these other threats.

So the bottom line is we do not have that insight into their operational- and tactical-level work. We retained a view of that strategic force which makes them an existential threat, but we lost contact with the operational and the tactical.

And in order to determine that we need to move forces into position that might change the outcome of the studies that you are referring to we need to have that capability and capacity of intelligence to reestablish indications and warnings so that we can deploy quickly the NATO Very High Readiness Joint Task Force, or deploy quickly the U.S. IRF [Immediate Response Force] to have them in position before or possibly to deter a conflict, and that might change some of the outcomes of what you are talking about.

So it is incredibly important for the first part of your question that we reestablish our ability to see and interpret so that we can deploy early to hope to avoid conflict or to change the outcome of the conflict.

Secondarily, as I said before, I believe that we will never go back to where Europe was when Captain Breedlove went there in 1983. Two corps, seven divisions, multiple brigades, 10 fighter wings—it was a force to be reckoned with. We will never go back there. This is not the Cold War.

But I do believe we are not where we need to be now in the mixture of permanently forward-stationed forces, prepositioned stock so that we can rapidly fall in on it. And then as you mentioned at the last part of your question, we are not where we might need to be to be able to penetrate with A2AD—anti-access and area denial environment that would allow us to do the third part, which is rapidly reinforce.

So just 20-second wrap up: I believe that we need to move forward in what our forward forces are, forward in how much prepositioned stock we have so that we don't have to have as many forward forces, and we need to make sure that we have the capacity to do anti-access/area denial to break it so that we can continue to rapidly reinforce.

I hope I answered your question, sir.

The CHAIRMAN. Mr. Courtney.

Mr. COURTNEY. Thank you Mr. Chairman.

And thank you. General, for your leadership and your thoughtful testimony here today.

On page 4 of your written testimony you advocate that the U.S. should join the United Nations Convention on Law of the Sea treaty, UNCLOS. I find that kind of striking because yesterday your colleague, Admiral Harris, who is dealing with a totally different part of the globe and totally different set of issues in terms of maritime contest, made precisely the same recommendation. And I was wondering if you could sort of describe what you think the benefits would be if we took your advice and ratified UNCLOS and what are the hindrances that you are dealing with today by not being part of the convention.

General BREEDLOVE. Sir, thank you for the question. I think our uniformed military has been pretty consistent over time in the support of the UNCLOS.

If I could just do a vignette for you of the Arctic. We are facing a very challenging situation in the Arctic. The Arctic, I think, should be an opportunity. As the ice flow pattern changes, the maritime trade route in the Arctic shortens by over 30 days, I am told, transit to the Far East. That should be an opportunity.

Many of our NATO allies, Canada, and the U.S. are concerned about what we see as the militarization of the Arctic now by Russia. What we would see in the Crimea situation and the Duma situation, currently in Syria, is that Russia has a pattern of putting military force in the field to set the conditions to negotiate from a position of power.

And so what we see now in the Arctic is Russia establishing a military capability and capacity to influence that new passage in the north. And being part of the UNCLOS would allow us to be at the table in the diplomatic, informational, and economic arenas to address that.

Last week I think, sir, you saw that Russia changed its claim in the North Pole area. It didn't affect U.S. claims, but it affected three of our other allies' and partners' claims. And these are the kind of things that will be severed in the framework of the UNCLOS.

Mr. COURTNEY. Thank you.

Again, I think we learned again the harm recently when the Hague Convention denied the U.S. request to intervene on the Philippine claims in the South China Sea—again, a trend that I think really mirrors what you are talking about, militarizing a part of the Pacific. And our inability to even be at the table when these issues are being resolved that will have a direct impact in terms of military strategy and resources in the future, you know, is the ultimate unforced error. So thank you for your input this morning on that issue.

Admiral Stavridis, when he was here a couple weeks ago, talked about the fact that the undersea realm is getting much busier, said, you know, highest level of activity since the Cold War. Do we have enough assets in terms of naval resources—submarines, antisubmarine, surface ships in terms of the European Command to address that issue?

General BREEDLOVE. So, sir, I am glad you asked that in the context of the European Command. I wouldn't want to try to advise you on the CNO's [Chief of Naval Operations] business on numbers.

But these undersea assets are a very highly sought-after asset. I will just factually say I did not get what I have asked for, and what that means is that in the North Sea in the vicinity what we call the GIUK gap—Greenland, Iceland, U.K. gap area—where all of the sophisticated submarines and surface combatants that Russia has comes out of the bastion area where they are built, tested, and fielded, and then employs in the Atlantic, in the Mediterranean, and some of transits to the Pacific.

But the bottom line is in that very contested, very highly sophisticated part of the world we play zone defense. We can't play man-on-man. And so I hate to simplify this, but it is just a very simple way of understanding.

Mr. COURTNEY. Thank you.

Again, our fleet today of attack subs is about 52 and, as I think you know, it is going to dip just because of the legacy fleet going offline. And, I mean, I guess we would probably agree that that is just going to make that stress even worse for your successors, in terms of trying to get those—the assets you need to play zone defense, let alone man-to-man.

General BREEDLOVE. And, sir, I would just—and not to change the question or to divert, but this is similar to other stories in what we call low-density, high-demand requirements: high-end ISR [intelligence, surveillance, reconnaissance], high-end aircraft, certainly submarines, et cetera, et cetera.

The CHAIRMAN. Mr. Rogers.

Mr. ROGERS. Thank you, Mr. Chairman.

General, it is good to have you back in front of us. Thank you for your service, and I don't think the administration has announced who is going to follow you but you are going to be tough to follow and I appreciate all you have done for our country.

General, do you have an opinion as to whether you believe Russia has any intention of returning into compliance with the INF [Intermediate-Range Nuclear Forces] Treaty?

General BREEDLOVE. Sir, thank you for the question and I am going to answer it in the way I answer a lot of things. I am unable to ascertain and I don't think I am qualified to really determine what Mr. Putin and his folks intend, but what I would say is that what I have done—and I have said this to you before—I look at what our opponent does as far as building capabilities and capacities, and then I infer from that how he would use them or what he might do with them.

And I think you have heard me testify before, as have many others, that we firmly believe that Russia is in violation of the INF Treaty, and that not only are they in violation of the INF Treaty but the type of weapons system that they have tested and fielded in that category is very easily hidden or masked in its conventional forces. And so it is worrisome to me that they have created a capability that will be very problematic for us to keep track of.

Mr. ROGERS. How do you think we should raise the cost to Russia for its violations?

General BREEDLOVE. Sir, the Secretary of Defense has laid out his approach to that and it is an escalating approach starting with diplomacy and then moving to more what I would call kinetic means. And I believe that we are in the phase where we are—we and our allies are trying to reach a diplomatic solution to that. But I support the Secretary of Defense framework for addressing the breach in the INF.

Mr. ROGERS. What do you think Russia is trying to hide from us in Kaliningrad by illegally denying our flights over this heavily militarized piece of Russian territory?

General BREEDLOVE. So Kaliningrad, sir, as you know, is a very militarized piece of property. And as we talked about just a little bit before, in this discussion of anti-access/area denial, A2AD, as we shorten it, Kaliningrad is a fortress of A2AD. It projects land attack cruise missile capability; it projects coastal defense cruise missile capability; and it projects air defense capability; so a complete bubble to defend against land approach routes or land targets, air targets, and seaborne targets.

And as I mentioned before, some of the land attack cruise missile systems or land attack missile systems in Kaliningrad are those that can be dual-use, meaning they can be nuclear. And I would not guess what they are trying to hide, but there are a lot of things in there that support these capabilities.

Mr. ROGERS. Lastly, you made reference in your opening statement to Russia weaponizing the migration from Syria. Can you speak more specifically to that?

General BREEDLOVE. Sir, I cannot—again, I look at what I see in capabilities and capacities and I determine intent. So what I am seeing in Syria in places like Aleppo and others are what I would call absolutely indiscriminate, unprecise bombing, rubblizing major portions of a city that do not appear to be—to me to be against any specific military target because the weapons they are using have no capability of hitting specific targets. They are unguided, dumb weapons.

And what I have seen in the Assad regime from the beginning when they started using barrel bombs, which have absolutely no military utility, they are unguided and crude, and what are they designed to do is terrorize the public and get them on the road; later, Assad using chlorine gas and other chemical-type approaches to these same barrel bombs. Again, almost zero military utility, designed to get people on the road and make them someone else's problem—get them on the road; make them a problem for Europe to bend Europe to the will of where they want them to be.

And so I see a continuing pattern in Aleppo and other places of this indiscriminate use of military capability that all I can determine from it is the goal is to get more people on the road and make them a problem for someone else to bend the will of those being affected.

Mr. ROGERS. Thank you, General.

I yield back.

The CHAIRMAN. Very disturbing.

Mr. Ashford.

Mr. ASHFORD. Thank you, Mr. Chairman.

General, thank you very much. We had the opportunity a few weeks ago to—in conjunction with the trip to the Gulf States, to stop at NATO headquarters and be briefed, and much of what was said there is what you have suggested today. And I want to thank you for the efforts to get the other NATO partners to contribute the 2 percent. I think you had a great deal to do with that and it is such a big deal.

And also the shift in the last 2 years in how we approach Russia, the threat of Russia, is much to do with your efforts, so I really—you know that, but I want to thank you again for that.

One of the discussion points at NATO headquarters really was the discussion about the treaty itself, about Article 5, about—is—in your view, does the language of that agreement, which was—or that treaty, which is relatively older now—a little younger than me, but older—is the language sufficient as we look at the types of threats that you have described, whether it is cyber or whether it is little gray men or it is a different kind of situation?

How close to Estonia do the Russians have to be or if there is some sort of cyber activity or other kinds of activity like that? At what point does it trigger? And that is my question.

General BREEDLOVE. Sir, thank you for that. And if I could just wind the clock back a little bit to the other articles of the treaty. We often talk about Article 5; as important to me is Article 3 and Article 4.

Article 3 can be summarized very succinctly in defense begins at home, and we have been using that with our allies and partners to talk to them about just what you said: increasing and thickening their own defense, investment in their own country. And that investment is not only 2 percent in total, but what is also important is that 20 percent of that needs to be recapitalization of investment in kit. It is not helpful if the entire portfolio is in personnel costs. And so Article 3—important.

Defense begins at home, and we have been working with allies and partners to build capabilities that fit nicely into the alliance. Everybody doesn't need to be flying F–16s. Some people need to be creating tactical air control parties, rotary-wing lift, et cetera, et cetera. So molding the alliance via Article 3.

Article 4, of course, is that point at where the nation feels threatened and begins a conversation with the other nations about, "We are facing a threat and how are we going to respond?" And this is the point when the nations are starting to look at and say, "This is a legitimate breach of what NATO was built to do—collective defense."

And then Article 5, of course, is the most highly recognized one. To your point, the language is not precise when it comes to what we now call sort of the gray areas: the cyber, the hybrids. And Mr. Putin is trying to live below that Article 5 level. He is taking action in nations now all around his periphery, trying to remain below that level at which the alliance would respond.

That is tough. It is tougher in the states between Russia and NATO, but I think he is already taking these actions in some NATO nations.

I would encourage maybe your staff to look at Mr. Gerasimov's model, his strategy of indirect action and deterrence. It is completely unclassified and out there on the Net, and if you look at his stage one, two, and three and what the actions he prescribes in that model of war, he is already taking those actions in many of our nations.

Mr. ASHFORD. Thank you, Mr. Chairman.

The CHAIRMAN. Thank you.

Mr. Franks.

Mr. FRANKS. Well, thank you, Mr. Chairman.

General, thank you for coming before this committee again. I understand this might be your last time before this committee, so if you will forgive me I would like to just take a moment and express my personal gratitude to you for being the noble and benevolent leader you have been on behalf of human freedom in this country, and I know my 7-year-old children have a better chance to walk in the light of freedom because of people like you.

And I truly believe that on just the basis of this committee's perspective that you have been a strategic asset in the arsenal of freedom, and I can't express to you just the personal goodwill I have for you and your family.

With that, in your opening statement—or your written statement—you talk a lot about the assurance and deterrence missions you accomplished under the umbrella of Atlantic Resolve. And it is my understanding that Atlantic Resolve is really not a named operation. What additional authorities and resources could you tap into if Operation Atlantic Resolve were a named operation?

General BREEDLOVE. So, sir, thank you. And thank you for your support of—Luke Air Force Base in Arizona, which is dear to my heart, but also to our military forces.

So the difference between the operation itself—and a named operation is subtle but important. Named operations have funding streams, they have dedicated rules of engagement, they garner certain priorities and allocations of forces, et cetera, et cetera. And so a named operation would bring more stability and long-term focus to Atlantic Resolve.

We are thankful to this committee and others for 3 years—or 2 years and possibly a third year—of ERI, which is very important to Atlantic Resolve because it pays for those rotational forces and things that explain we are a part of the way forward. I think a named operation would give a sustained funding stream to things like that.

Mr. FRANKS. You also mentioned that EUCOM does not yet have the personal—personnel, equipment, and resources necessary to carry out its growing mission. And to me that implies that although there is a plan for the future, that if a military crisis were to break out in there tomorrow, that you would not be equipped to deal with it as you would see fit.

So what specific resources do you need to fulfill your missions which are not included in the current budget? And secondarily, is your headquarters adequately sized and staffed at the levels required for you to execute your mission?

General BREEDLOVE. So, sir, if I could step back just to piggyback on a thought that I put out before, for 20 years we have been trying to make a partner out of Russia and we have changed our force structure and our headquarters and other capabilities in Europe to reflect a mission that was about engagement and building partnership capacity.

Now we have determined that we—people categorize it differently, but we definitely do not have a partner in Russia. And our resolve now is to be able to meet the challenge of a resurgent, revanchist, however you want to label it, Russia.

We have to be able now to be a warfighting headquarters and a warfighting force, as opposed to an engagement and partnership-building capacity force. We will still do those functions, but we have to rethink, do we have the capability and capacity to be a warfighting force? And we do not.

And I think that we have got to look at our forward force structure; we have got to look at our prepositioned capability; and we have got to make sure we have the access to Europe in the face of A2AD. That will take capacity and it will take some new capabilities.

And as to the headquarters, our Secretary—Assistant Deputy Secretary of Defense has recognized that our headquarters is not sized right. We are still downsizing the headquarters from the BCA [Budget Control Act], first $478 billion cuts. We had 5 years' worth of cuts to the headquarters laid in. We are still getting smaller. But this year the Deputy Secretary has increased our headquarters size to stop—to arrest that, and hopefully we will continue to do that across the next years.

But it will take some time to reconstitute a warfighting headquarters from where we have been for the last 20 years.

Mr. FRANKS. Well, thank you.

Thank you, Mr. Chairman. Mr. Chairman, I hope that this committee and this country have the opportunity to access the wisdom and acumen of this gentleman in the future.

The CHAIRMAN. Appreciate it.

Mr. Moulton.

Mr. MOULTON. Thank you Mr. Chairman.

And, General, thank you very much for your service.

Are we meeting Russia's threat in the Arctic, from your perspective in Europe? Are we adequately meeting the militarization of the Arctic today?

General BREEDLOVE. I am going to try to answer this question along the following lines: I do not believe that our nation, nor most of the other nations of the Arctic Council, wants to militarize the Arctic.

Mr. MOULTON. Well, I agree with that.

General BREEDLOVE. But what we see is that our opponent has decided to militarize the Arctic. And so I think this is again a discussion of do we have the appropriate capabilities of all manner—aircraft, icebreakers, other things—and do we have the capacities? And that is work that is being looked at now. I think——

Mr. MOULTON. From your assessment today, do you believe that we have those capabilities and capacities to meet and deter Russia's activity in the Arctic?

General BREEDLOVE. In the Arctic? We do have some extremely capable Arctic capabilities, as do some of our allies.

In fact, just before arriving here for this series of engagements with Congress I was in Alaska and we were talking about this with the leadership in Alaska and the forces of the ALCOM [Alaskan Command] there, and they do specialize in these capabilities. The real question is we have to determine what the capacities that are required are.

Mr. MOULTON. General, moving on to a different topic and back to Representative Ashford's question, some experts have said that now we have to afford additional policy authority to DOD [Department of Defense] to allow for training of National Guard, other forces, to counter the little green men and little gray men in Eastern Europe. How can this be best accomplished and what changes to statute or what policy provisions would better enable that kind of cooperation?

General BREEDLOVE. Sir, I am going to be very honest. I don't think I can answer it the context of how you asked it, but I do believe I can address this issue.

Mr. MOULTON. Okay. Okay.

General BREEDLOVE. So the capacity to address hybrid warfare in its many forms—and it is bigger than little green; as you have heard, we also talk about little gray men, meaning that hybrid warfare goes across all four elements of national power—diplomatic, informational, military, and economic. And so leaving the nations where they are and helping them to determine what they need to do is important, and I will get to the part that is important to you.

For instance, if you look at the three Baltic nations from north to south, they do things very differently. This hybrid approach in one nation is almost completely a military problem and very slightly a ministry of interior problem. In another of the nations it is about 50/50, ministry of defense, ministry of interior. And then the other one is exactly opposite; it is almost entirely ministry of interior and partly ministry of defense.

So I think where your question is heading is, as you know, we have unique title 10 limitations of what we can do with other nations, so it is an all-of-government engagement. The National Guard brings some interesting capabilities, when you have guardsmen who have experiences in other fields—for instance judiciary, legal——

Mr. MOULTON. Sure.

General BREEDLOVE. And so I think that is where this may have headed.

Mr. MOULTON. So, General, do you think that we need to revise the current policy to be able to do that kind of training, to better meet this hybrid warfare or whatever you want to call it threat from Russia?

General BREEDLOVE. Sir, I don't think I know—or I am not familiar with the limitations enough to pass judgment. But let me tell you, as a commander I need the ability to engage a government across all the elements of government power to train them to address the hybrid war.

Mr. MOULTON. That is very helpful, General. I think my concern is that, as you said, we are never going to get to the seven divisions that we had in the Cold War, and we can expend all our resources trying to incrementally move in that direction, which may be headed in the right direction, but if [we] expend all our resources doing that and don't get to a point where it adequately does deter Putin at the expense of all these other aspects of this warfare we are going to really miss the boat.

General BREEDLOVE. I completely agree that we have to have capacities in all of those elements of national power to deter, as we have talked about with Congresswoman Davis.

Mr. MOULTON. Thank you, General.

Thank you, Mr. Chairman.

The CHAIRMAN. Thank you.

Dr. Fleming.

Dr. FLEMING. General, I want to thank you for testifying before us today and, once again, thank you for your sage counsel and ad-

vice and all your years of experience and what you have brought
to the table. You will be sorely missed. Everything you said I think
is spot-on to where we need to be in terms of deterrence and dealing with an emerging Russia.

I do have some questions. I told you earlier with respect to B–
52s, Barksdale Air Force Base is in my district, home of Global
Strike Command and General Rand, and so I want to know from
you, what is the deterrence effect of the B–52 bomber? What do you
see as the future for that bomber in terms of what it can bring to
the battlefield both in kinetic action but also in deterrence?

General BREEDLOVE. Sir, I will not dodge your question, but I
would say this is much more appropriately addressed by General
Welsh and others as to that specific platform. But let me tell you
what the bomber—and the B–52 being a mainstay of that fleet—
the bomber brings to deterrence.

And that is as you know the B–52, the B–1, and to a certain de-
gree the B–2 have become much more flexible across their lives.
And the B–52 as a platform for employing all manner of weapons
like the other bombers, but certainly the B–52 is a great deterrent
effect because it can be a part of a purely conventional response to
try to de-escalate the situation, which is what we really want.

We don't want to fight. We want the capacity and capability to
defeat, but we don't want to go there. And so the ability of that
particular platform to be able to do all missions and bring capacity
to both a conventional and a non-conventional war is important.

The other piece is it has proved, as you know, to be an incredibly
long-living airframe with capability still into the future. I am not
sure if it is still true, but when I was the vice chief of staff at the
Air Force now 5 years ago we used to say that the mother of the
son or daughter that will be the last pilot of the B–52 has not been
born yet.

Dr. FLEMING. Right.

General BREEDLOVE. And it will be well over 100 years old before
we are done with it.

Dr. FLEMING. Yes. Amazing.

Well, and since you brought that up, we are looking at the devel-
opment of the Long Range Strike Bomber [LRS–B], so my question
is what will be that effect and what are the current timelines for
both the upgrade to B–52 and replacement of long-term strike
bombers?

General BREEDLOVE. So, sir, as you remember, we were talking
earlier about A2AD—anti-access/area denial. One of the biggest
keys to being able to break anti-access/area denial is the ability to
penetrate the air defenses so that we can get close enough to not
only destroy the air defenses but to destroy the coastal defense
cruise missiles and the land attack missiles, which are the three
elements of an A2AD environment.

One of the primary and very important tools to busting that
A2AD environment is a fifth-generation ability to penetrate. In the
LRS–B you will have a platform and weapons that can penetrate,
key to the future in the—of the older generation bombers and platforms are developing, and we are and have those weapons that can
penetrate. And so those upgrades are all important to me as a user

so that I can call on the service to bring forward the capabilities and capacities to address A2AD.

Dr. FLEMING. Right. Great. Thanks.

And in the remaining time I have, could you comment on the current state of research by the Navy and Air Force into deterrence assurance? By this I mean the gaming scenarios in planning to address the aggressive behavior and Russia's apparent shift in nuclear doctrine.

General BREEDLOVE. So I can't speak specifically to just the services. You may be familiar with what we call the RSI, the Russian Strategic Initiative. It is modeled after the CSI, the Chinese Strategic Initiative, which is nearly 7 years old. As we in the past couple of years have seen Russia as no longer a partner we have developed the Russia Strategic Initiative to do just this kind of work, to look at the things we need to change in weaponry, but more importantly, to do things like war gaming to understand how they would react to our war plans, et cetera, et cetera.

So what I am aware is as the leader of the Russia Strategic Initiative for the Department of Defense, we are getting some very exquisite help in understanding this business.

Dr. FLEMING. Great. Well, thank you, General, and so much for the Russian reset.

And I yield back.

The CHAIRMAN. Mr. Langevin.

Mr. LANGEVIN. Thank you, Mr. Chairman.

General, I want to thank you for your testimony today and for your service to our nation. Your service has been absolutely invaluable to our country and we will miss you in your retirement. But I certainly want to be among the many to wish you well in this next chapter of your life.

Officials within the Department have stated that they are very worried that our military's ability to counter and wage electronic warfare has atrophied pretty significantly while other partners around the world—or I should say adversaries around the world—have invested heavily in this area, and that we may be lagging behind countries such as Russia. Would you agree with this assessment, and how do you believe EUCOM is currently positioned to address this challenge across the AOR [area of responsibility]?

My other question that I have I hope we can get to is—and I spend a lot of time obviously on cybersecurity, and you mentioned that the challenges that we face in that space with respect to what Russia is doing. And my question is, how do you believe that we are doing at countering cyber threats with our allies against what Russia is doing and what their capabilities are? And do our NATO allies see eye to eye on this threat, and are our partners' capabilities mature enough to manage the dangers that—and challenges that we are seeing across cyberspace?

General BREEDLOVE. Thank you, sir.

On the electronic warfare the same sort of situation applies. For 20 years we have been making a partner out of Russia so our focus has not been on the capabilities that they have been developing. And secondarily, again, for all the right reasons for the last 13 or so years our nation's military has been focused on counterinsurgency operations, COIN, in Afghanistan and fighting Al Qaeda in some of the spaces around the world.

And so we have been focused very deeply on addressing a threat that does not have electronic warfare capability. So while we have retained capability, we have not really practiced to it to the veracity that we used to, nor have we retained the capacity that might be required to bust these growing A2AD problems we see around the world.

So to really shorten the answer up, we have electronic warfare capability; we probably do not have the capacity we need now to address it. Our suppression of enemy air defense capabilities, SEAD, to take down air defense nets and things are very good but they are not dense. We don't have a lot of them.

Russia knows how we roll and they have invested a lot in electronic warfare because they know that we are a connected and precise force and they need to disconnect us to make us imprecise.

When it comes to cyber, this is, sir, I think a glass well over half-full. When I arrived to my station about 3 years ago I think that many of the nations of the alliance and in Europe were very insularly focused. They were acknowledging the cyber threat but they were worried primarily about their own cyber problem.

What we discovered, though, is with 28 nations in alignment in an alliance you may have an absolute iron curtain wall around two or three of them, but there are 25 other doors into the enterprise. And so what we had to do is come to a larger, more corporate approach to cyber.

And, sir, I see that happening. I am encouraged by what I see happening.

I would recommend that someday in your travels you stop into Estonia and go to the NATO cyber center in Tallinn. It is absolutely superior and they are adding value to our alliance every day.

Mr. LANGEVIN. Thank you, General.

Next question: Is there a role for the U.S. and for EUCOM to play in assisting our European allies to mitigate the potential national security threats when it comes to the ongoing refugee crisis? What does that role look like and what resources are needed?

General BREEDLOVE. Sir, there is a role and we are executing that role now. The refugee crisis and the part that we are addressing the most is that embedded in this refugee flow is criminality, terrorism, and foreign fighters. We have adopted and built a very good network of sharing information, sharing intelligence, and trying to target and understand these flows of criminals, terrorists, and foreign fighters as they move back and forth, and so we are a part of that now.

As you are aware, the NATO alliance began an operation in the Aegean Sea essentially just about a week ago where we are beginning to try to help our Greek and Turk allies to address the dense flow of refugees across that water space by being a part of managing that water space in terms of surveillance and reconnaissance and handing off data to the coast guards of Turkey and Greece. It is a little more complicated than that, but we have—the NATO alliance has begun to enter into that portion of the mission as well.

Mr. LANGEVIN. Thank you, General, and thank you again for your service. We wish you well.

General BREEDLOVE. Thank you, sir.

The CHAIRMAN. Mr. Nugent.

Mr. NUGENT. Thank you, Mr. Chairman.

And I definitely want to thank General Breedlove and his staff for your honest answers in the prior meeting that we had. It is very sobering to hear where we are and without illusion.

I worry as we move forward. You know, we have done this now pivot to Asia, rebalance in the Pacific, all those types of things, and I think we are trying to do, unfortunately, way too much in regards to the stresses that we are putting on the military.

You know, there was a point in time where our policy was to be able to fight, you know, two major conflicts while, you know—but what we found is that we had a hard time doing one when you look back at Afghanistan and we had to have, you know, forces there for 15 months on a single rotation.

And so I think that we are fooling sometimes the American public to think we have the—I know we have the desire and I know that we have the best trained, best equipped force on the face of the Earth. But I don't know that we have enough, and I think we hit that on capacity, that we have enough to do the things that we told the American people that we can do and should do.

I think we have been really I guess hiding the ball in regards to hoping that our adversaries don't see that, and I truly have a lot of—I believe that Mr. Putin is very calculating and is not stupid by any stretch of the imagination.

But I guess the question is, you know, back when I first ran 6 years ago it was a big deal about, "Hey, listen we need to get out of Europe; we need to let the Europeans deal with their issues." And I think while that sounded good at the time, obviously now we are paying a dear price for that.

So why is it so important? And we need to stress this to the American public because everyone is footing the bill. Why is it so important that we have permanently stationed—forward-stationed troops and equipment in Europe? Why is it that important that we should invest that?

General BREEDLOVE. So, sir, thank you for the question. And just a 30-second recap: I believe that permanently forward-stationed troops are a part of that mixture.

Mr. NUGENT. Correct.

General BREEDLOVE. We have to have the appropriate amount of permanent-stationed, the appropriate amount of prepositioned so that we can rapidly reinforce, and then we need to have the capability and capacities to be able to rapidly reinforce to include busting this A2AD problem. So the permanently forward-stationed forces are an important part.

And here are some things that are not often heard. Permanently forward-stationed forces buy you a lot of things. One of them is relationships, and relationships equal access.

The flexibility that our—many of our nations, but let me just mention a few—that Spain, Italy, Greece, and even Turkey—the flexibility that they give us to move around and employ forces to address problems across all of North Africa, the Levant, and even to support CENTCOM [Central Command] into Syria and Iraq, this is all built on relationships and trust that are established over time by permanently stationed forward forces. I cannot overstate the importance of having these—this access.

A couple of sort of quippy remarks that I will give to you. One is that you cannot surge trust. You cannot surge relationships. If we are not in a nation, establishing trust and relationship, and then when we desperately need to be able to do execute force from or within that nation you don't—you can't surge the trust or the relationship.

Mr. NUGENT. And doesn't having permanently stationed forces buy us time to do just what you are talking about? When you have prepositioned equipment it buys us time to actually get to that equipment?

General BREEDLOVE. It does. It does, and that is why it is a mix. The permanently forward-stationed forces are there, ready, and can execute. They are ready to fight forward if they have to, and that allows—enables the prepositioning and enables the capability to respond.

Mr. NUGENT. So do we have enough prepositioned—or not prepositioned, but do we have enough permanently stationed troops in Europe?

General BREEDLOVE. Sir, I am on record multiple times as saying no. We are looking at that now, but if we choose not to increase permanently stationed forces forward then we can adjust and pick up the requirement in the rotational force.

Mr. NUGENT. But hasn't it been a problem in regards to—and I know we—and I'm getting gaveled out on this one—but in regards to when you have different commands flushing through that you don't have a continuity?

General BREEDLOVE. Right. This is a problem that could manifest itself. Our U.S. Army and Navy and Air Force, by the way, in their rotation patterns are dedicating units. It will not always be perfect, but we have units assigned with a primarily European mission that are a part of that rotational force. We are trying to address just your concern.

Mr. NUGENT. I appreciate it.

And I appreciate the Chair. Thank you for very much.

The CHAIRMAN. Ms. Duckworth.

Ms. DUCKWORTH. Thank you. I am actually going to continue the gentleman's line of questioning because we were thinking along much of the same ways.

General, thank you again so much for being here. I want to pick up on this line of questioning.

You know, the fiscal year 2017 budget request quadruples the amount of the fiscal year 2016 request for the European Reassurance Initiative, but a lot of that is for prepositioning of equipment in Central and Eastern Europe, and for heel-to-toe rotational deployments. I was reading the National Commission on the Future of the Army's report that has two significant recommendations. One is to forward station an ABCT [armored brigade combat team] in Europe itself, whereas the other has to do with the aviation, the CAB [combat aviation brigade].

And I want to sort of peel back the layers of the effect of the Army's Aviation Restructuring Initiative and what it has done to our aviation capability in Europe. Specifically, you know, we go back to this idea of building trust and long-term relationships. One, let me start off by saying—am I right in saying that you would prefer to have permanently placed ABCT and additional equipment in Europe? Would that be a true statement?

General BREEDLOVE. Yes, ma'am.

Ms. DUCKWORTH. Okay. So on the aviation side, the report actually suggests that the rotational model will work except that we need more of a warfighter-aligned headquarters. What is there now is really more of an administrative aviation headquarters as opposed to a CAB-type of headquarters there that would actually be much more aligned to that rotational mission, they can come in, they can pick up. Would you agree with that?

General BREEDLOVE. So, ma'am, the report I think correctly identifies the absolute value of having a dedicated command and controlled force. And frankly, it just emphasizes the value in general of Army aviation as one element of air power in Europe. And they are all absolutely critical.

Ms. DUCKWORTH. They are. Thank you. I am not promising anything, but I would hope that with such an increase in the ERI funding that we might be able to address some of the aviation shortfall.

Can you talk a little bit more about the rotational model on your aviation needs in Europe? And where have you assumed specifically the most risk and what capability gaps needs the most attention when it comes to Army aviation?

General BREEDLOVE. So, ma'am, what I need to do is give some thanks and respect to what the Army did as they took the last tranche of aviation out of Europe. If you look at it in a net way, we really didn't lose any presence because the aviation that we had in Europe at the time was continually being tasked into theater. So while it was assigned in Europe it was gone a fair amount.

A larger piece left Europe, but the rotational piece that we got to replace it is dedicated to Europe and does not rotate into theater. So it netted out almost exactly the same in the amount of time that we had aviation on the ground. So I need to—we need to properly acknowledge the Army's efforts to make this right for Europe.

But the larger picture is that faced with the revanchist, resurgent Russia, we do not have the aviation requirement that we need in Europe, and that will be the focus of my command into the future.

Ms. DUCKWORTH. Okay. And so you are actually saying—are you saying then that you would like to have a full—a CAB permanently stationed in Europe?

General BREEDLOVE. Ma'am, the planning is ongoing. It may be more than a CAB. I would not want to put a number on it now and have it exactly wrong when the planning is finished.

Ms. DUCKWORTH. Okay. I only have a minute left. Can you comment a little bit on the State Partnership Program? Having been in the—spent my 23 years in the Illinois National Guard——

General BREEDLOVE. Cannot say enough about it.

Ms. DUCKWORTH. Since Poland is our country and they are staring down the barrel of Russian aggression there in Poland——

General BREEDLOVE. The State Partnership Program, 21 States, 22 nations, is one of my premiere tools. I hate to use a word like that, but literally they represent 23, 24 percent of the engagement that I have in Europe.

I have told this committee a couple of times that I much prefer permanently stationed forces, rotational forces being an acceptable but second option.

I would recategorize a little bit the State Partnership Program. They are a rotational force. They are a bit episodic. But the difference is that they maintain long-term relationships in leadership, in command, in training.

Forces are going left to America, right to Europe, and the—most of these programs are wildly successful. Some of them are just successful. But the point being that this is a very valuable tool in our quiver to be able to develop capacity in our allies, especially the smaller, former Soviet allies, et cetera, et cetera.

Ms. DUCKWORTH. And I thank you for service to this country, General.

General BREEDLOVE. Thank you, ma'am.

The CHAIRMAN. Mr. Jones.

Mr. JONES. Mr. Chairman, thank you.

And, General, thank you. As everyone else has, you are a great military leader and we appreciate it more than we could ever tell you.

Yesterday on the floor of the House, Mr. Brooks, who just left a few hours ago, gave a very disturbing speech on the fact that America is headed toward Greece financially. I later came along to give another 5-minute speech about the waste of money in Afghanistan, talked about the fact that John Sopko said that, to the Senate, that our country, Department of Defense spent $6 million to buy nine goats from Italy to send to western Afghanistan.

I wonder, when I listen to you, and—because I have such great respect for your evaluation of Russia and the threat that they could bring to more of Europe than it does today. Then I think about the comment by Admiral Mullen when he was Chairman of the Joint Chiefs when he said, "The biggest threat to our military is the growing debt of our nation."

I listen to you and your recommendations and the things that you feel like we need to do not only in Europe but for our military, but specifically Europe today that we need to do to be a stronger deterrent in Europe. My concern is that I have read recently that a couple of the civilian leaders in a couple of the countries have debated reducing the amount of money going into the defense budget of some of those countries.

You, having relationships that you have had both with military leaders and civilian leaders, do you feel—talking about the civilian leaders now, not the military leaders—that they fully understand that they have got to make a financial investment as much as America has to make to keep Europe safe from being taken over by Russia?

General BREEDLOVE. Sir, thank you much. And if I could just comment that I have deep respect for Admiral Mullen. I have worked for him a couple of times directly in my life and he is a man of, I think, incredible character, and he really has it upstairs.

The answer to the last part, which is the focus of your question, is we need to have a sober reply. But I have said that I am a glass half-full——

Mr. JONES. Right.

General BREEDLOVE [continuing]. Here.

In Wales we made a commitment—we being the nations of the alliance—made a commitment to get towards the 2 percent. They gave themselves a broad time period, which, you know, was a little bit worrisome—10 years. But they made a commitment to get to 2 percent. What I have seen is because of the continued aggressive behavior of Russia the nations have become much more focused on this.

And I have used these three numbers a couple of times. They are exactly wrong. They change, but they are pretty close to right: 16 of NATO's nations have stopped the decline in their budget; 5 of NATO's nations are already at 2 percent—we need to qualify at least one of those and I will mention that in a second; and then I believe—this is Phil Breedlove's opinion, not others—that there are about 7 nations that have I think a legitimate plan to get to the right spending in a reasonable amount of time, not 10 years but 4, 5, 6 years.

And so I think I would use those numbers to point out to you sir, that I do believe the leadership of the nations are beginning to make decisions with their budgets. I do not want to overstate be- cause there is a lot here to do. And as I mentioned earlier, one of the important things in the 2 percent is that it is important and the other goal is that 20 percent of that 2 percent is on recapital- ization investment so that they can bring capability to the table. If the entire budget is a personnel budget it is not going to be helpful over time as a force. And so we also need to bring focus among our allies and partners that they not only get the invest- ment up, or certainly arrest the decrease, but they also need to look at the investment accounts to make sure that they are bring-ing capabilities to the fore.

But I just want to close with it is not perfect. A lot of work to do, but I am over half-full here because of what I see in these trend lines.

Mr. JONES. General, thank you so much.

I yield back.

The CHAIRMAN. I was just looking; we are at 26 percent, accord-ing to the last chart we have up here, on the monetization part. So we got a little work to—have a little work to do.

Ms. Stefanik.

Ms. STEFANIK. Thank you, Mr. Chairman.

And thank you, General Breedlove, for being here to testify and for your service and leadership to our nation.

I am interested to hear your thoughts on the increased online presence of ISIL in Europe and our capacity to truly counter these threats at the combatant command level. How is EUCOM leverag-ing technology and new ideas to counter online propaganda and equipment as it relates not only to the hybrid threat posed by Rus-sia but also this increased online recruitment and digital propagan-da that we are seeing by ISIL in Europe?

General BREEDLOVE. So I would categorize this in two ways. We are not where we need to be yet. We have a lot to do. We have started and are headed in the right direction.

I am sure you will have Admiral Rogers here from NSA [National Security Agency]/Cyber Command to talk to you. He has been a magnificent partner in that he has taken the approach of pushing capacity and capability to the combatant commanders so that the combatant commanders can individually focus and target that capability and capacity.

In this open forum I will have to stop there on what that looks like, but let me assure you that the admiral has a wonderful focus on how he is going to do this for us, but it is—we have a lot farther to go.

Inside of EUCOM itself, again, in an open forum I will tell that we have several venues where we are using exquisite tools to get after this problem set. And I will just stop there. Again, not enough yet, but we have started this process.

Ms. STEFANIK. So as much as you can say in an open forum, what tools do you need? How will increased ERI funding assist in the area? Broadly, can you give us guidance?

General BREEDLOVE. So, ma'am, ERI is more focused on our allies and how we fight there, and so I will have to have my staff get back to your staff. I don't want to misstate.

I am not sure that there is this specific capability. There are capabilities in cyber, but what you are talking about I cannot definitively speak to that. I will have my staff contact your staff on that——

Ms. STEFANIK. Great.

General BREEDLOVE [continuing]. Rather than misstate.

[EUCOM has contacted Rep. Stefanik's staff and will provide a briefing in response to her questions.]

Ms. STEFANIK. Let me shift to another area. A mission as complex as EUCOM requires a great deal of international partnership and interagency communication. How well, in your assessment, is EUCOM integrated with the various agencies throughout Europe to counter the increased threats, and would you say there is a solid unity of effort between partners and agencies to counter the challenges posed by a resurgent Russia and the various unconventional threats that face Europe today?

General BREEDLOVE. Ma'am, this is a place I am very proud of our command. We are well integrated. And partially that is because this committee made decision years ago to develop a distinct branch of our command called J9 where we pull in all of the other agencies. It is a little mini agency. And we pay for their presence in order to ensure that we have connections to law enforcement, FBI [Federal Bureau of Investigation], and a lot of other agencies which we will not mention here.

But we know that in Europe when we try to combat things like foreign fighter flows and terrorism—in Europe this is not about kinetic strikes like it is in Afghanistan, Iraq, Syria, and portions of North Africa. In Europe this is about integrating with the highly capable legal, judicial, and police systems of Europe. And so we have invested distinctly in this capability to have connective tissue to the other nations of Europe.

And so this is a place where EUCOM before my time—I do not take the credit except for that we have expanded it and continued to fund it before me—but leaders before me have seen the wisdom and the value of this interagency approach in Europe.

Ms. STEFANIK. Great. Thank you very much.

I yield back, Mr. Chairman.

The CHAIRMAN. Thank you.

Ms. McSally.

Ms. McSALLY. Thank you, Mr. Chairman.

Thank you, General Breedlove, for your service and commitment to our troops and to our security. You have talked many times about the force structure and our downsizing in Europe. I think back at one point we had I think six A–10 squadrons in the U.K. back in the day, then we went to one at Spain, and less than 3 years ago that one closed down.

We are now deploying A–10 units of the nine remaining operational across the active Guard and Reserve for part of the ERI in order to help with training and deterrence. So that is just one example, but that was just a couple years ago.

Can you give some insight into the logic? That is an entire capability, because now there is none there, that we have lost.

And I am still waiting to hear about from the Air Force as the cost comparison of stations that are full-time versus rotating over. But can you give some insight as to that logic, and do you think looking in hindsight that was not a good decision?

General BREEDLOVE. So I will allow the Air Force to talk to you about cost-benefit ratio.

Ms. McSALLY. Right——

General BREEDLOVE. As a user I am just looking for the capability.

And I think, you know, I—the round number that my staff gave me is that we are—we have about two A–10 exercises and about 200 flying hours a month on average now in EUCOM. So we are asking for that capability.

I try to refrain from asking specifically for airframes; I try to ask for capabilities. And certainly we have airplanes that can deliver what the A–10 delivers, but the A–10 is extremely good at delivering——

Ms. McSALLY. I mean, just based on your overall testimony, though——

General BREEDLOVE. Right.

Ms. McSALLY [continuing]. Would it be better to have a capability like that stationed in Europe versus rotating over, just in line with everything that you said?

General BREEDLOVE. So what we have seen is that that capability serves a very important niche of our requirements.

Ms. McSALLY. Great. Thanks.

You may not be able to answer the next question but a recent RAND study, looking at defense of the Balkans, talked about, among other things, a, you know, lack of air superiority because of just the swift nature of that potential scenario. You said you were looking into force structure options, but if you were not resource-constrained and you had everything you wanted, could you give a sense or can you get back to me with a sense of what would the fighter force structure look like in order to make sure we have air superiority.

It has been now 60 years since the last time we did not have air superiority in any military operation so——

General BREEDLOVE. April 1953——

Ms. MCSALLY. Exactly.

General BREEDLOVE. So yes, ma'am. We do not at present have sitting on the ground in Europe sufficient capacity——

Ms. MCSALLY. Right——

General BREEDLOVE [continuing]. To ensure air superiority over the battlefield. We would have to start off any conflict working towards localized air superiority to employ troops and then reinforce from the rear.

If I could, I would actually attack this question a little differently. The premiere aircraft in air superiority these days are not only air superiority platforms but they are explicit, stealth, precision, attack platforms.

And these kinds of capabilities are incredibly important to busting that A2AD problem that we have talked about several times today, not only to provide air superiority for the troops but that stealthy ability to deliver precise weapons to take down A2AD is incredibly important. And it will take a significant amount more of that capability to establish what you and I have known to be air superiority over the battlefield.

Ms. MCSALLY. Yes. Could we maybe get back in a classified setting about what that—like how many—what would that look like? What would the force structure look like? What——

General BREEDLOVE. So, as you know, we are working our war plan through the business now, and that will allow us to definitize that. It is not ready for primetime yet.

Ms. MCSALLY. I have just got about a minute left. Obviously we have talked about the challenge of our partners not reaching 2 percent of their GDP [gross domestic product] and their spending. It seems like the awareness level is going up and some turning around, but it is still not enough.

If we compare the—with the PACOM [Pacific Command] theater, you know, our allies see the value of us being there for their own defense and they often support in other ways, even if it is not just with the military. They are paying the bills; they are providing that monetary support.

Are there other initiatives we could push a little harder on right now, now that we have got the Russian threat, we have got the ISIS threat, to say, "All right, fine. If you are not ramping up your military capability, you are going to start paying some of the bills for us to be here so that we can free up resources for other things" just to be a little more creative and have them step up their contribution.

General BREEDLOVE. As you know, in limited ways that has already happened in a couple of places. And as I mentioned before, it is not perfect. We need more. But what we really see, especially in the Mediterranean nations, is the flexibility that they allow us to move forces around, especially to meet the threat in North Africa, is quite demonstrative.

I asked someone once, "Would you—what would happen if another nation asked to come into your state and on a routine basis move around large groups of foreign military and foreign aircraft, and sometimes do that on less than 48 hours' notice?" And so I think we have to acknowledge that there are some sacrifices these nations are making.

Ms. McSALLY. They get value out of it too.

Thank you, Mr. Chairman.

The CHAIRMAN. General, do you know off the top of your head how many permanent U.S. military installations we still have in Europe?

General BREEDLOVE. I do not. The number of new major installations is less than two dozen, but there are a lot of small ones.

The CHAIRMAN. Yes. Okay. Thank you.

One other question I want to ask you with your NATO hat on that has not been raised today is Turkey. You know, we read every day about the tensions related to this Syria situation especially, and so from a NATO perspective what is that relationship like with Turkey today as it integrates into the alliance?

General BREEDLOVE. So, Mr. Chairman, let me say unequivocally in a mil-to-mil environment, which is where I am most qualified, it is a strong and remaining strong relationship. Of course, the position of the military inside Turkey has changed over time, but our mil-to-mil relationship is strong.

We don't always see perfectly eye to eye, but we have incredible cooperation and personal relationships. The chief of defense there, General Hulusi Akar, is not American-trained but he is Western-trained and he really understands the way we do business, and he has—he is a very much a cooperative partner.

Turkey, as you know, Mr. Chairman, lives in a really tough neighborhood: to their south a civil war that is really going quite badly; to the north the Black Sea, which has become a bastion of Russian power—again, one of the three major A2AD nodes that we have talked about. And so Turkey is in a tough place and facing what they see are some tough problems around them.

But let me assure you, I feel only qualified to speak to the mil-to-mil piece. We have a strong and continued relationship mil-to-mil with our ally Turkey.

The CHAIRMAN. Well, we have seen in other cases where that continuation of a strong military relationship is really the bedrock as governments come and go that our relationships can often depend on, so I think that is a very important thing for us to keep in mind.

General BREEDLOVE. Nineteen major installations, Mr. Chairman.

The CHAIRMAN. Thank you, sir, I appreciate that. I often get asked at home why don't we close some bases in Europe, and so that is—helps arm me with the facts.

General, I have got to warn you that you have received lots of accolades today and people saying they are going to miss you. The problem is even this week we have had interactions with two former combatant commanders and picking their brain, so we don't usually let people get off too lightly or completely away from us.

And we may see you again before the change of command, but thank you very much for being here today and for your insights. And with that, the hearing stands adjourned.

[Whereupon, at 11:41 a.m., the committee was adjourned.]

APPENDIX

February 25, 2016

PREPARED STATEMENTS SUBMITTED FOR THE RECORD

FEBRUARY 25, 2016

Statement of Ranking Member Adam Smith
HEARING ON
**Full Spectrum Security Challenges in Europe and
Their Effects on Deterrence and Defense**

February 25, 2016

Over the last several years, the security environment in Europe has grown more complex. Our allies and partners in Europe face a number of threats on multiple fronts. For example, instability in the South from the crisis in Syria, the movement of foreign fighters, and the substantial threat of terrorism as we have seen in the wake of Paris and other disrupted plots across Europe. Further, we continue to see Vladimir Putin's destabilizing actions in eastern Europe. Confronting these challenges requires continued, focused, cooperative support with our European allies and partners.

For nearly two years, Russia has occupied Crimea and has fomented the continuing separatist struggle in eastern Ukraine. Additionally, we've seen in recent days renewed fighting between Ukraine and Russian-backed separatists in eastern Ukraine, and persistent tension has led to repeated failures to adhere to a ceasefire agreement. As we note concerns for European security and sovereignty, one primary question to consider is: what more can be done to address the conflict in Ukraine and to provide our Ukrainian partners with the support they need in supplies, training and support for governance—especially to root out corruption—that will ultimately improve and solidify their security? How can we best facilitate full implementation of the Minsk agreements?

Russia's destabilizing efforts continue, and it seems clear that Russian aggression and malign influence in Europe will likely be issues that the United States and our partners in Europe will have to grapple with for years to come. It is in our interests and the interests of our allies and partners to increase our preparedness for deterring Russian aggression, to align our defensive posture accordingly, and, if necessary, to respond appropriately. Secretary Carter recently stated: "While we do not desire conflict of any kind" with Russia, "we also cannot blind ourselves to the actions they appear to choose to pursue."

This year, the Administration has requested $3.4 billion for the European Reassurance Initiative (ERI)—a quadrupling of last year's request—to reassure our European allies and partners facing the threat of Russian aggression. Over half of which, $1.9 billion, is proposed for prepositioned equipment. This "Army Prepositioned Stock" includes tanks, heavy artillery, weapons, ammunition, and other essential warfighting materiel that is difficult to transport in a timely manner. I understand the Administration intends to strategically place this equipment throughout Europe with the goal of reducing reaction time needed for U.S. personnel to respond to urgent crises. These prepositioned sets would enable the United States to focus primarily on transporting military personnel to areas of contention and allow U.S. service members to simply "fall in" on their military equipment when they arrive. It is important to support Europe against Russian aggression and we will strive for an appropriate balance regarding our European flexible force presence, combined exercises, prepositioned hardware, infrastructure, and the building of partner capacity. To meet capability needs, members of the North Atlantic Treaty Organization (NATO) should also work to increase their defense spending to meet the NATO target. To be clear, the best defense of Europe is a strong collective defense.

Our NATO and non-NATO partners are essential to America's security. It is also important to focus on our cooperation beyond Europe. We share a commitment with our European partners and with NATO to oppose and combat ISIL and terrorism in the Middle East and North Africa. European states, possibly more than most, are fully and soberly aware of the persistent threats posed by instability and extremism in North Africa. Further, we should remember that NATO members are playing an essential role in training, advising, and assisting the Afghan National Security Forces as they provide for their own security.

General Breedlove, as you conclude your time in command, I want to thank you for your work to enhance cooperation with our European partners and prepare us to move forward together toward a more capable posture to address the challenges to security in Europe.

HOUSE COMMITTEE ON ARMED SERVICES

STATEMENT OF GENERAL PHILIP BREEDLOVE
COMMANDER
U.S. FORCES EUROPE
February 25, 2016

I.   Introduction

As I arrive at the end of my assignment as both Commander of U.S. European Command (EUCOM) and Supreme Allied Commander for Europe (SACEUR), I have had no greater honor in my 39-year career than to lead the Soldiers, Sailors, Airmen, Marines, Coast Guardsmen and civilians of EUCOM. These remarkable men and women continue to serve not only in the EUCOM theater, but put themselves in harm's way across the globe and I thank this Committee for its continued support to them and all our nation's armed forces.

I cannot overemphasize how important European nations, in particular our NATO Allies and non-NATO partners, are to ensuring America's security and safety. Many of our most capable and willing Allies and partners are in Europe, playing an essential role in promoting our vital interests and executing a full range of military missions. In this time of increasing military and strategic risk, we will continue to seize this opportunity to further strengthen the Transatlantic Alliance as EUCOM continues to experience unprecedented instability in an area of the world we once viewed as whole, free, prosperous, and at peace.

Europe is not the same continent it was when I took command, as new threats and challenges continue to emerge. EUCOM's steady state operations, activities, and actions, alongside our European Allies and partners, are targeted at meeting these challenges to ensure our national security interests, including defending our nation forward from conventional, asymmetric, and even existential threats emanating from our Area of Responsibility (AOR).

EUCOM continues to play a vital deterrence role, against state and non-state actors alike, in support of the U.S. military's larger global strategy. The forces forward deployed in this theater operate across Europe, the Middle East, and Africa. Likewise, the forward operating bases in Europe provide the U.S. Joint Force with essential access in the Mediterranean and the Levant, as well as North Africa and the Arctic.

Our theater priorities and supporting activities in Europe fully support both the National Security and the National Military Strategies. First and foremost they support our national direction to counter malign Russian influence and aggression, as well as meet our enduring interests – the security of the United States; a strong U.S. economy; respect for universal values at home and abroad; and a rules-based international order.

However, it is not enough to simply have a strategy that supports our national security objectives; we also require resources in the theater necessary to accomplish these objectives.

Since the release of the 2012 Defense Strategic Guidance and our national decision to rebalance to the Asia/Pacific region, EUCOM has paid a steadily increasing price in resources and assigned forces to help achieve rebalance. During the height of the Cold War, there were over half a million U.S. personnel assigned in the European theater. Today that number is around 62,000 permanent military personnel, of which 52,500 are in direct support of EUCOM missions. The remaining personnel support the missions of other organizations, such as U.S. Africa Command (AFRICOM), U.S. Transportation Command (TRANSCOM), and NATO. EUCOM-assigned forces are now tasked with not only the same missions we have performed for the past several decades but with a substantial increase in our deterrence and reassurance operations in response to Russian occupation of Crimea and its aggression in eastern Ukraine, as well as requirements in the U.S. Central Command (CENTCOM) and AFRICOM AORs. EUCOM conducted Operation ATLANTIC RESOLVE (OAR), trained Ukrainian National Guardsmen and defense forces, provided resources in support of AFRICOM's counter-Ebola mission and continued to provide critical support of CENTCOM's counter-ISIL mission. It is important to understand the critical roles these permanently stationed forces and bases play in this theater

In response to the new European security environment, I have strongly advocated for, and our Defense Department, Administration, and Congress have supported, not only suspending further drawdown of this theater, but now the need to look at tailored, supportable increases in capabilities as we requested in the FY 2017 budget.

II. Theater Assessment

The U.S. and NATO face two primary threats to our security interests: Russian aggression and growing instability on our southern flank. Russia continues to foment security concerns in multiple locations around the EUCOM AOR. Concurrently, we deal with a variety of transnational threats that largely emanate from instability in Iraq, Syria, North Africa, and the rise of the Islamic State of Iraq and the Levant (ISIL). The U.S. and NATO must take a 360-degree approach to security – addressing the full-spectrum of security challenges from any direction and ensure we are using all elements of our nation's power.

A. Russia

For more than two decades, the United States and Europe have attempted to engage with Russia as a partner by building military, economic, and cultural relationships. During the 1990s, Russia became a Partnership for Peace member with NATO, signed the 1994 Budapest

Memorandum, and endorsed the 1997 NATO-Russia Founding Act. The text and tone of these instruments presumed Russia was a partner who shared our commitment to security, prosperity, and inclusive peace in Europe. With these Russian commitments, the Department of Defense made security and force posture determinations significantly reducing European force structure based on the assumption that Russia was a sincere partner and in 2009, the United States sought to "reset" its relationship with Russia, which had been damaged by Russia's 2008 invasion of the Republic of Georgia.

Despite these and many other U.S. and European overtures, it is now clear Russia does not share common security objectives with the West. Instead, it continues to view the United States and NATO as a threat to its own security. Since the beginning of 2014, President Putin has sought to undermine the rules-based system of European security and attempted to maximize his power on the world stage.

Russia continues its long-term military modernization efforts, and its recent actions in Ukraine and Syria demonstrate an alarming increase in expeditionary force projection and combat capability and logistical sustainment capacity. Russia has spent the past 20 years analyzing U.S. military operations and has established a doctrine and force to effectively counter perceived U.S. and NATO strengths. In examining the threats Russia poses to NATO and the U.S., we should consider Russian actions comprehensively, taking into account their capabilities, capacities, and intentions.

To the north: Arctic region. Increased human activity is changing the way the United States, one of the eight Arctic nations, views the Arctic. EUCOM, along with our Allies and partners, is working to contribute to a peaceful opening of the Arctic. We strive to prevent and deter conflict, but we must be prepared to respond to a wide range of challenges and contingencies. We work with our Allies and partners to ensure the Arctic is a stable, secure region where U.S. national interests are safeguarded and the homeland is protected.

Decreasing sea ice is increasing commercial and recreational activity in the high north. In the EUCOM AOR, shipping activity along the Northern Sea Route (NSR) is providing shorter alternatives for cargo. The unpredictability of weather and ice between seasons makes the Arctic a harsh environment for commercial shipping; however, the trend is clearly toward less Arctic ice and longer shipping windows.

The eight Arctic states have a solid history of cooperation in the region. This includes the 2011 Arctic Search and Rescue Agreement, signifying an important step in Arctic cooperation. However, we cannot ignore Russia's increase in military activity which concerns all nations—not just those in the Arctic. Russia's behavior in the Arctic is increasingly troubling. Their increase in stationing military forces, building and reopening bases, and creating an Arctic military district – all to counter an imagined threat to their internationally undisputed territories – stands in stark contrast to the conduct of the seven other Arctic nations.

Russia's improvements to Arctic settlements are ostensibly to support increased shipping traffic through the NSR. However, many of these activities are purely military in nature and follow a recent pattern of increasingly aggressive global posturing. We continue to encourage all of our Arctic partners to respect the broad and historical agreements against militarization of the high north and remain dedicated toward maintaining a peaceful opening of the Arctic.

Under the United Nations Convention on the Law of Sea (UNCLOS), several Arctic states are submitting extended continental shelf claims. Joining the Convention would allow the United States to submit own our claims, promote U.S. interests in the environmental health of the oceans, and give the United States a seat at the table when rights vital to our national interests are decided. Cooperation among the Arctic states and adherence to the UNCLOS legal framework will deter escalation in the Arctic.

To the east: Russia and periphery (Ukraine and Baltic States). The Kremlin views the current situation in Ukraine as unsettled and a critical point of long-term friction. Russia's coercive use of energy has grown with threats and outright use of force. Eastern and Central European states, to include the Baltics, are concerned about Russia's intentions in Europe and consider Russia's aggression in Ukraine validation of their concerns.

Russia's aggressive foreign policy toward Ukraine and the Baltic States amplifies a general sense of unease among NATO's eastern flank members, with tensions across the region, both inside and outside NATO, exacerbated by Moscow's illegal occupation of Crimea and direct support for combined Russian separatist forces in eastern Ukraine. Kremlin efforts to establish levers of influence in the Baltics across the diplomatic, economic, information, and security spectrum are meant to develop an environment favorable to Moscow and present an ongoing challenge to Western efforts aimed at assuring these NATO Allies.

<u>Russian use of Unresolved Conflicts as a Foreign Policy Tool</u>. Describing the prolonged
conflicts in states around the Russian periphery as "frozen" belies the fact that these are on-going
and deadly affairs often manufactured by Russia to provide pretext for military intervention and
ensures the Kremlin maintains levels of influence in the sovereign matters of other states.

- <u>Georgia</u>: A clear purpose motivating Russia's invasion of Georgia in August 2008 was to
  prevent Tbilisi from pursuing its sovereign decision to become a full member of the
  European and transatlantic communities – a decision endorsed by NATO in the Bucharest
  Summit Declaration. In the aftermath of the 2008 war, Russia recognized Abkhazia and
  South Ossetia's independence, and Russia's military still occupies the regions. In an attempt
  to create additional obstacles to Georgia's Euro-Atlantic integration, Russia also signed so-
  called "treaties" of alliance with Abkhazia and South Ossetia to increase its military,
  political, and financial control over these regions. Moreover, Russia has continued its policy
  of "borderization" along the Administrative Boundary Lines separating the two territories
  from the rest of Georgia by building fences and other physical barriers. In coordination with
  the de facto authorities in Abkhazia and South Ossetia, Russian border guards prevent
  freedom of movement of Georgian citizens into the territories and obstruct unfettered access
  for international and humanitarian organizations.
- In Moldova, Russian forces have conducted "stability operations" since 1992 to contain what
  is described as a separatist conflict in Transnistria. Moldova remains disappointed with
  Russia's continued political, economic, and informational support to the separatist regime.
  Most upsetting to Moldova is Russia's military presence (1,500 troops) on Moldovan
  territory, which is aimed at maintaining the status quo in the region. Moldova has two
  battalions (150 personnel each) and one company (120 personnel) permanently deployed on
  the peacekeeping mission in the security zone of the Transnistrian Region.
- Regarding Armenia and Azerbaijan, Russia is part of the Minsk Group process, aimed at
  resolving the Nagorno-Karabakh (NK) conflict. Despite this, Moscow has actually increased
  instability in the region by selling arms to Azerbaijan while maintaining a troop presence in
  Armenia. In fact, violence along the Line of Contact and the Armenia-Azerbaijan border has
  escalated significantly in the last two years, with 2015 being the deadliest year in the conflict
  since the ceasefire was signed in 1994. The complicated NK conflict is arguably the greatest
  impediment to the spread of peace and security through Europe to the Caucasus.

Russia modulates these conflicts by manipulating its support to the participants, while engaging in diplomatic efforts in order to preserve its influence the affected regions. Just as the Soviet Union dominated the nations of the Warsaw Pact, Russia coerces, manipulates, and aggresses against its immediate neighbors in a manner that violates the sovereignty of individual nations, previous agreements of the Russian government, and international norms.

Other unresolved conflicts in Europe require persistent attention to keep them from escalating. In the Balkans, Serbia's continued reluctance to recognize Kosovo's independence detracts from regional stability and security. Kosovo also struggles with interethnic tensions between Kosovo Serbs and Kosovo Albanians, while fledgling government institutions, unlawful parallel government structures, and a weak rule of law contribute to high levels of corruption, illicit trafficking, and weak border security. NATO's Kosovo Force, supported by EUCOM, plays an essential role in ensuring a safe and secure environment and freedom of movement and is respected by both Kosovo and Serbia.

Russian Support to Syria. Russia's military intervention in Syria has bolstered the regime of Bashar al-Assad, targeted U.S.-supported opposition elements, and complicated U.S. and Coalition operations against ISIL. The Syrian crisis is destabilizing the entire region, and Russia's military intervention changed the dynamics of the conflict, which may lead to new or greater threats to the U.S. and its Allies for years to come. Moscow's ongoing operations in Syria underscore Russia's ability and willingness to conduct expeditionary operations and its modernized military capabilities which are emboldening the Kremlin to increase its access and influence in a key geopolitical region.

B. Threats to European Allies and Partners

ISIL and Other Threats Coming from the South. Numerous terrorist attacks have taken place in the EUCOM AOR over the past year, including the near simultaneous attacks in Paris that killed approximately 130 people this past November, with several additional disrupted plots targeting U.S. forces and interests. Over the past 12 months, ISIL has expanded its operations throughout the EUCOM AOR, formally declaring an expansion of its self-declared "caliphate" into the Caucasus while conducting multiple attacks across the region. ISIL uses social media and online propaganda to radicalize and encourage European extremists to travel to Syria/Iraq or conduct attacks in their home countries. We anticipate additional European terrorist attacks in the future. From Paris to Copenhagen, Belgium to Turkey and the Caucuses, ISIL and Al-Qaida inspired terrorists have conducted attacks that tear apart the fabric of free and democratic societies. These terrorists are not geographically limited to Europe. ISIL elements have conducted multiple attacks against European individuals and interests in North Africa including the Sinai. While we expect ISIL terrorists in North Africa will remain focused on internal issues in Africa in the near term, they may pose a greater threat to Europe should they achieve a safe haven in Libya or another North African country.

Similar to ISIL, Al-Qaida and its affiliates in the Middle East, North Africa, and Asia, such as al-Qaida in the Arabian Peninsula and al-Nusrah Front, possess the ability to conduct mass casualty attacks against U.S. and Allied personnel and facilities in Europe. Complicating this picture are self-radicalized terrorists who, with little guidance from parent organizations, pose an unpredictable threat.

Left- and right-wing politically inspired violence. Internal dissent also threatens our partners in Europe. As an example, leftist groups such as the Kurdistan Workers Party (PKK) and the Revolutionary People's Liberation Party/Front (DHKP/C) in Turkey remain a persistent threat to both the Turkish government and U.S. interests. DHKP/C was responsible for the August 2015 small-arms attack outside the U.S. Consulate in Istanbul and the February 2013 suicide attack at the U.S. Embassy in Ankara.

Refugee crisis. Europe is facing a historic refugee crisis as displaced persons, primarily from Syria, Afghanistan, Iraq, and unstable parts of Africa flee conflicts and attempt to reach Western European countries such as Germany and Sweden. Over 1 million refugees or economic migrants arrived in Europe in 2015, entering primarily in Italy and Greece with 2.6 million refugees residing in Turkey. These figures have trended upward for the past two years and will likely continue to rise in 2016 as the conflict in Syria continues.

There is a concern that criminals, terrorists, foreign fighters and other extremist organizations will recruit from the primarily Muslim populations arriving in Europe, potentially increasing the threat of terrorist attacks. Also, local nationalists opposed to a large-scale influx of foreigners could become increasingly violent, building on the small number of attacks against migrant and refugee housing observed to date.

The refugee crisis is tragic, and the nations in the European Union are taking steps and adding resources to increasing humanitarian assistance to conflict affected countries while expanding domestic security measures and pursuing diplomatic solutions to the growing problem and its root causes. EUCOM work with our interagency partners to monitor this humanitarian situation.

Foreign Terrorist Fighters (FTF). Foreign terrorist fighters remain a key concern for EUCOM and our foreign partners. Over 25,000 foreign fighters have traveled to Syria to enlist with Islamist terrorist groups, including at least 4,500 westerners. Terrorist groups such as ISIL and Syria's al-Nusra Front (ANF) remain committed to recruiting foreigners, especially Westerners, to participate in the ongoing Syrian conflict. The ability of many of these Europe-originated foreign fighters to return to Europe or the U.S. makes them ideal candidates to conduct or inspire future terrorist attacks.

European Economic Challenges. The growing instability in Europe fueled by a revanchist Russia is occurring while most of the continent remains stagnated in a persistent financial crisis, anemic economic growth, and continued energy dependence. The Greek economic crisis that nearly led that country to leave the 'euro zone' in the summer of 2015, is unfortunately indicative of the wide European debt crisis that at one time threatened the health of the European economy, which is unambiguously linked to the U.S. economy. Continued weak economic growth not only keeps unemployment rates high, specifically among young migrants susceptible to radicalization, it also hinders European countries' ability to increase defense spending, resulting in most NATO countries remaining below the two percent NATO benchmark. European continued dependence on Russian energy, specifically former-Soviet and eastern-bloc states, only serves to bolster Russia's ability to coerce those nations to achieve political gains.

Challenges for NATO. As NATO undergoes a profound historical change, it is both performing its core tasks of cooperative security, crisis management and collective defense and is recommitting to the basics, emphasizing Articles 3, 4, and 5 of the Washington Treaty.

Article 3 commits Allies, through "self-help" and "mutual aid," to develop "their individual and collective capacity to resist armed attack." It reminds us that defense begins at home, that all members must contribute to collective defense, and that each nation has a responsibility to maintain their capability for their own defense. Poland is a good example of an Ally who has reformed its military structure and is modernizing its military to meet the security needs of both itself and NATO.

Article 4, highlights the fact that Allies may consult together when the security of any of them is threatened. While it has only been invoked five times in the six decades since NATO's creation, spurred by events in Ukraine and Syria, three of those have come in the past four years. Aside from these Article 4 consultations, NATO practices consultation on an almost daily basis.

Article 5 is the most known and understood Article and it emphasizes the responsibility of Allies to respond collectively to attacks on any member state. As declared by the Heads of State and Government at the Wales Summit, the events of the past two years have reminded us all of our responsibilities to each other and that "the safety of our citizens and protection of territory is the foremost responsibility of our Alliance." In response to a changed security environment, NATO is adapting its processes, increasing its responsiveness and renewing its focus on collective defense by enhancing the Alliance's deterrence and defense posture, including increased awareness, resilience, readiness, solidarity, and engagement. Even so, additional work needs to be done to improve intelligence sharing and indicators and warnings among NATO members.

NATO's ability to perform its core tasks is underpinned by the capabilities provided by each member state. It is publicly acknowledged by all Allies that defense spending, in support of the right capabilities, must increase. While there is much to be done by all Allies to ensure the needed capabilities are present for today's strategic environment, there are some promising trends. In 2015, 21 Allies halted or reversed declines in defense investment as a percentage of GDP, and 24 halted or reversed declines in equipment investment as a percentage of defense investment. Five Allies met the 2% of Gross Domestic Product guideline in 2015, compared to just three in 2013. Eight Allies allocated the NATO guideline of 20% or more of their defense budgets to equipment in 2015, up from four in 2013.

III.   **Executing EUCOM Missions**

On any given day, EUCOM forces throughout Europe are engaged in a variety of activities to deter Russia, and counter the threats posed to our Allies and partners. These missions include: (1) training and exercising of our forces in order to be ready, if called upon, to conduct full spectrum military operations; (2) assuring our Allies of our commitment to collective defense; (3) training and collaborating with our NATO Allies and partners to maintain interoperability; and (4) working with our Allies and partners to effectively prepare for and support disaster relief operations.

In addition to my responsibilities as a warfighting commander, I also often serve in the role of a supporting commander. EUCOM forces are ready to support the needs and missions of four other Geographic Combatant Commanders, three Functional Combatant Commanders, and numerous Defense Agencies. This includes the ability to appropriately base and provide logistics support functions to forces assigned to operations in the AFRICOM and CENTCOM areas of responsibility.

A. Deter Russia

Russia's continued aggressive actions and malign influence remain a top concern for our nation and my highest priority as EUCOM Commander. The cease fire in eastern Ukraine remains tenuous at best, and Russia continues its destabilizing activities in direct contravention of the Minsk agreements. Russia also shows no signs of engaging in dialogue over its illegal occupation of Crimea, and seems intent on transforming this situation into a permanent redrawing of sovereign boundaries in Europe. While the U.S. and European nations have responded with diplomatic and economic sanctions, Russia continues its aggression in eastern Ukraine by providing personnel, equipment, training, and command and control to combined Russian-separatist forces. EUCOM, along with Allies and partners, continue to contribute to Ukraine's efforts to build its own defense capabilities, including providing training for Ukraine's armed forces. It also continues to destabilize countries throughout its periphery. We must not allow Russian actions in Syria to serve as a strategic distraction that leads the international community to give tacit acceptance to the situation in Ukraine as the "new normal." Shortly after Russia's illegal occupation of Crimea, our immediate focus was on assuring our Allies, through Operation ATLANTIC RESOLVE, of our steadfast commitment to NATO's Article 5 provision on collective defense. Now that we are nearly two years into this operation, our efforts are adding a deterrence component with the goal of deterring Russia from any further aggressive actions. These supporting roles tax the capacity of EUCOM's assigned forces, straining our ability to meet other operational requirements.

As the Department continues to refine a holistic U.S.-Russia defense strategy, events in Europe continue to evolve. As a result of emergent requirements, EUCOM has undertaken a number of assurance and deterrence measures that will continue throughout 2016 and are greatly expanded in the fiscal year (FY) 2017 Budget request.

European Reassurance Initiative (ERI). ERI continues to provide the additional funding that allows us to increase our assurance activities throughout the EUCOM AOR. EUCOM believes that the strategy of assuring our NATO Allies and Partners while seeking to deter Russia from further aggression, as undertaken by the Department, through ERI has significantly helped EUCOM with the dynamic security challenges within the AOR. We are grateful for the strong congressional support of this initiative that reassures and bolsters the security and capacity of our NATO Allies and partners. With your continued support, we will use FY17 ERI request to expand deterrence measures against Russian aggression. As an example of assurance measures, the U.S. Army deployed an Armored Brigade Combat Team (ABCT) set of equipment (known as the *European Activity Sets* (EAS)) to the European theater. EUCOM is currently distributing Company and Battalion sized elements of the equipment along NATO's eastern border. This equipment is used by the Army's regionally aligned force personnel for the purpose of training and exercising with our Allies. Storing and maintaining EAS equipment in this manner helps reduce transportation time and costs and reassures Allies and partners in the region of our steadfast commitment.

With the FY17 ERI submission, EUCOM supports the Army's effort to increase *Army Prepositioned Stocks* (APS) unit sets to increase deterrence. This set of equipment helps shorten the response time in a time of crisis. EUCOM plans to use existing infrastructure for APS unit set storage and maintenance to the maximum extent possible, to include former locations used by the United States for this purpose. New locations, however, may be needed given the 80% reduction of European infrastructure over the past 25 years and NATO's expansion along its eastern boundary.

The United States, along with its NATO Allies, will continue to take actions that increase the capability, readiness, and responsiveness of NATO forces to address any threats or destabilizing actions from aggressive actors. Over the last 15 months we have helped NATO members better defend themselves, along with non-NATO partners in the region, who feel most threatened by Russia's actions against Ukraine. Continued congressional support sends a clear message to the Russian leadership the United States is wholly committed to European security.

Reassurance Measures. Operation ATLANTIC RESOLVE supports the mission to assure and defend NATO, enhance our Allies' and partners' abilities to provide their own security, and deter further Russian aggression. EUCOM engagement, training, exercise, and cooperative activities will continue to support enabling regional cooperation with our Allies and partners to address the challenges on Europe's eastern and southern flanks, and the threats emanating from and within Europe. These activities will enable the timely generation of fit for purpose forces, capable of addressing common and collective security challenges within Europe.

Russia Strategic Initiative (RSI). A Russia staunchly committed to challenging international norms is not just a EUCOM security challenge, but a challenge for the entire Department of Defense. We need look no further than its ongoing intervention in Syria and the serious operational implications it presents CENTCOM. Accordingly, we are addressing this threat collectively across numerous Combatant Commands through the Russia Strategic Initiative (RSI). RSI provides the Combatant Commanders a framework for understanding the Russian threat and a forum for integrating and coordinating efforts and requirements related to Russia. RSI allows us to confront this immediate threat to ensure we maximize the deterrent value of our activities without inadvertent escalation. RSI also provides DoD an avenue to analyze the Russia problem set across the interagency, academia, and think tanks for broad perspectives on an extremely complex problem.

Strategic Messaging and Countering Russian Propaganda. EUCOM's strategic communications, information operations (IO), and related influence capabilities such as Military Information Support Operations (MISO) are the most powerful tools EUCOM has to challenge Russian disinformation and propaganda. Russia overwhelms the information space with a barrage of lies that must be addressed by the United States more aggressively in both public and private sectors to effectively expose the false narratives pushed daily by Russian-owned media outlets and their proxies. As part of the FY17 ERI request, EUCOM has requested the authority and appropriation to conduct IO. EUCOM will continue to increase its collaboration with Department of State, other agencies, partners, and Allies in order to effectively engage select audiences and counter malign actions and activities.

B. Support to Allies and Partners

Support to NATO. EUCOM is the visible symbol of the United States' commitment to the NATO Alliance. The Command serves as a key agent to build capabilities and conduct NATO operations. EUCOM will continue to support regional cooperation with our Allies to address the challenges within Europe as well as those coming from its eastern and southern flanks, enabling the generation of forces capable of addressing common and collective security challenges.

The Allies' commitment under Article 3 of NATO's Washington Treaty, with its dual principles of "self-help and mutual aid," provides the basis of EUCOM's security cooperation in support of NATO. EUCOM is a key enabler for the Alliance's unique and robust set of political and military capabilities to address a wide range of crises before, during, and after conflicts. EUCOM assists Allies in building security capacities, command and control, interoperability, and deployability to provide their own internal security, contribute to regional collective security, and conduct multilateral operations.

EUCOM also supports NATO's actions with crisis management, operations and missions. With the invocation of Article 4 consultations by Turkey and Poland in recent years, EUCOM has worked with other Allies through OAR, theater security cooperation programs, and air defense support to Turkey to provide a tangible Alliance response.

U.S. support to the continued implementation of NATO's Readiness Action Plan (RAP) is essential for a credible Article 5 deterrence. The RAP contains new operations plans, an enhanced NATO Response Force with quicker deployment times and assigned forces, new authorities for SACEUR, and an improved NATO command structure. The U.S. pledge to contribute key enablers is critical to the success of the Very High Readiness Joint Task Force (VJTF), while seven Allies (France, Germany, Italy, Poland, Spain, Turkey, and the United Kingdom) have committed to provide the lion's share of land force contributions. EUCOM has also continued its support to other key aspects of the RAP, including maintaining continuous presence in the eastern portions of NATO, establishing prepositioned supplies and equipment, enhancing the capabilities of NATO's Multinational Corps North East and Multinational Division South East, and the establishment of a NATO command and control presence on the territories of eastern Allies. Continued U.S. support on all of these efforts is essential to ensuring Allied cohesion and capability to meet our collective Article 5 commitment.

Missile Defense in Europe. EUCOM continues to implement the three phases of the European Phased Adaptive Approach (EPAA) and deepen our missile defense partnerships and assurances within NATO. Phase 2 of the EPAA, the first Aegis Ashore Missile Defense System (AAMDS), which is located in Deveselu, Romania, will provide enhanced medium-range missile defense capability, to expand upon Phase 1, which has been operational since 2011. While

EUCOM has benefited tremendously from the Phase 1 forward deployment of four Aegis ballistic missile defense (BMD) capable surface ships to Rota, Spain, this capability is greatly enhanced by the on-schedule completion in December 2015 of the AAMDS site in Romania, the final building block of Phase 2. EUCOM is working to certify the site's capability and ensure its interoperability with NATO command and control systems. To validate this construct, EUCOM and our NATO Allies will be conducting test and evaluation exercises, and we look forward to certifying our command and control interoperability, and delivering the key capability to NATO.

As we complete the work on Phase 2, EPAA Phase 3, which includes the second AAMDS at Redzikowo, Poland, is on track for completion in the 2018 timeframe. The basing agreement is complete and was ratified by the Polish Parliament by an overwhelming majority. The implementing arrangements are progressing on schedule, meeting both U.S. and Polish expectations, and Poland continues to invest heavily in preparing for the AAMDS deployment. Building upon Phase 1 and 2, the AAMDS site in Poland will support EUCOM plans and operations and represent the U.S. voluntary national contribution to NATO's missile defense of European populations, forces, and territory.

Within NATO, EUCOM is working with key Allies such as Spain and the Netherlands who continue to invest in air and upper tier ballistic missile defense, and are considering investment in capabilities which complement the U.S. Aegis ballistic missile defense capability. Another shared concern is defense of the Aegis Ashore sites.

To support other key allies, U.S. Army Europe's 10th Area Air Defense Command and 5th Battalion 7th Air Defense Artillery Regiment have been doing yeoman's work in their deployments to Turkey and supporting engagement and exercises with NATO, Poland, Germany, Romania, Israel, and many other nations. As their strikes in Syria have made clear, Russia presents a robust potential threat across the range of ballistic and cruise missiles from land, sea, and air. EUCOM requires the ability to protect our headquarters, bases, and forces. Since BMD forces worldwide are strained, EUCOM has diligently engaged with our Service components, fellow combatant commands, the Missile Defense Agency, and the Joint Staff to find solutions and drive future capability deliveries to address current and future threats. We ask for continued Congressional support in these efforts.

Cyber Operations. Emerging threats to national security, spurred by the global diffusion of information, advancements in technology, and a rapidly changing operational environment are impeding both U.S. and our Allies' ability to operate freely in the cyber domain. Both state and non-state actors have offensive cyber capabilities that can disrupt and damage weapon systems, platforms, and infrastructure throughout our AOR. Non-state actors are seeking to develop capabilities to conduct sophisticated cyber-attacks in the future and will likely pose an increasingly dangerous threat to our forces.

Our theater cyberspace supporting strategy is the foundation of all cyber operations in the EUCOM AOR and enables us to integrate cyber operations with the other warfighting domains to achieve campaign objectives. Among the Command's top priorities are the full implementation of Joint Information Environment (JIE) and a Mission Partner Environment (MPE). JIE is DoD's initiative to address the security, effectiveness, and efficiency challenges of the current and future Information Technology (IT) environment. MPE is DoD's initiative to enable operations with allies and other partners, both inside and outside of the DoD, in support of ongoing and future operations. While much more work must occur, EUCOM is already beginning to reap the benefits of these initiatives to enhance our mission effectiveness, improve cyber security and reduce risk to missions and our forces.

Nuclear Deterrence and Weapons of Mass Destruction (WMD). The supreme guarantee of Alliance security is provided by its strategic nuclear forces, particularly those of the United States. EUCOM collaborates closely with U.S. Strategic Command to assure Allies of the U.S. commitment to the Alliance, including, for example, bomber assurance and deterrence missions. NATO's 2010 Strategic Concept, 2012 Deterrence and Defense Posture Review, and 2014 Wales Summit Declaration all affirmed that deterrence, based on an appropriate mix of nuclear, conventional, and missile defense capabilities, remains a core element of our overall strategy, and that "as long as nuclear weapons exist, NATO will remain a nuclear alliance." Consistent with NATO's commitment to the broadest possible participation of Allies in the Alliance's nuclear sharing arrangements, EUCOM maintains a safe, secure, and effective theater nuclear deterrent in support of NATO and as an enduring U.S. security commitment within the EUCOM AOR. Through rigorous and effective training, exercises, evaluations, inspections, operations, and sustainment, EUCOM ensures that U.S. nuclear weapons and the means to support and deploy those weapons are ready to support national and Alliance strategic objectives.

WMD in the hands of a state or non-state actor, continue to represent a grave threat to the United States and the international community. Through our Countering WMD Cooperative

Defense Initiative Program, EUCOM executes bilateral, regional, and NATO engagements to bolster our collective capability to counter the proliferation of WMD (and their precursors) and mitigate the effects of a WMD event.

Foreign Fighters. The flow of returning foreign terrorist fighters to Europe and the United States poses a significant risk to our European forward-based forces and the homeland. Actively encouraged by ISIL, returning foreign terrorist fighters are mounting attacks, a problem that will magnify as the flow of returning individuals increases over time.

Our Allies and partners share these concerns. EUCOM works in conjunction with the Department of State, AFRICOM and CENTCOM to monitor and thwart the flow of foreign fighters going to and from Syria and the Levant, dismantle extremist facilitation networks, and build partner nation capacity to counter the flow of foreign fighters on their own. We are pursuing efforts bilaterally, regionally, and within a NATO construct to reduce the potential for successful terrorist attacks within EUCOM and at home. USAREUR has created a program called WOLFSPOTTER whereby they integrate various intelligence feeds and share those effectively with partners to assist in the identification of "lone wolf" actors more effectively.

Foreign Military Sales (FMS). Foreign Military Sales benefits not only interoperability with our Allies and partners, but also our defense industrial base, with defense articles and services totaling well over $5 billion per year in the European theater. From Israel to the Arctic, our FMS programs are improving Alliance capabilities and meeting the challenges associated with meeting NATO's capability targets.

FMS offers opportunities for the United States to improve the trends in European capability acquisition. Our Allies and partners understand the quality of our FMS program in comparison with other sources of defense articles and services, and seek ways to acquire our defense articles while balancing the requirements of the European Union and offers from other sources. Recognizing the quality we offer comes with a high price tag, EUCOM encourages our partners to engage in shared FMS actions by pursuing multi-national and multilateral FMS solutions in order to reduce costs for participants and provide opportunities to pool and share resources, increasing NATO capabilities across the theater.

EUCOM appreciates the various Congressionally-authorized Building Partner Capacity (BPC) programs which engage the FMS infrastructure to provide defense articles and services more quickly than traditional FMS, as illustrated by our actions in the Baltics and Ukraine.

These BPC processes are benefitting the readiness, capability, and interoperability of nearly all of our partners in Central and Eastern Europe.

C. EUCOM Support to NATO in Afghanistan

The continued operational and financial support of NATO and other partners is a crucial pillar of building sustainable security in Afghanistan. NATO has transitioned from International Security Assistance Force (ISAF) to the RESOLUTE SUPPORT Mission (RSM). Our European Allies and partners continue to bear the burden of providing the bulk of forces, second only to the United States. As we conduct RSM, EUCOM will continue to prepare our Allies and partners for deployments to support the train, advise, and assist mission. Authorities such as Global Lift and Sustain, "Section 1207" (loan of certain U.S. equipment to coalition partners), 10 USC 2282 (global train and equip authority), and the Coalition Readiness Support Program are absolutely essential for EUCOM to provide Allies and partners with logistical support and continued interoperability with U.S. and NATO forces. These authorities allow countries to receive much needed equipment such as intelligence, surveillance, and reconnaissance assets; interoperable communications gear; counter-IED and explosive ordinance disposal equipment; medical equipment; and night vision devices; as well as training to effectively use the equipment.

D. Assistance to Israel

A continued deterioration of security in the Levant region is a threat to the stability of Israel and neighboring countries. With limited warning, war could erupt from multiple directions with grave implications for Israeli security, regional stability, and U.S. interests.

EUCOM primarily engages with Israel through our Strategic Cooperative Initiative Program and numerous annual military-to-military engagements that strengthen both nations' enduring ties and military activities. The U.S.-Israel exercise portfolio includes major bilateral exercises and continued engagement resulting in renewed and strengthened U.S.-Israeli military and intelligence cooperation relationships. Through these engagements, our leaders and staff maintain uniquely strong, frequent, personal, and direct relationships with their Israeli Defense Force counterparts.

The direct threat to Israel by ballistic missiles and rockets with longer range and increased accuracy pose a significant challenge. EUCOM maintains plans to deploy forces when requested in support of the defense of Israel against ballistic missile attacks. EUCOM also conducts maritime BMD patrols and weekly training exercises in cooperation with Israel. The

U.S. and Israel have continued to execute the "Combined U.S.-Israel BMD Architecture Enhancement Program," which includes both exercises and dedicated test events managed by the Missile Defense Agency, all supported by EUCOM.

E. Support to other Combatant Commands

In addition to EUCOM's responsibilities as a warfighting command, it also must serve in the role of a supporting command.

EUCOM continues to provide direct operational support to AFRICOM by deterring growing opportunities for al-Qaeda and its affiliates and adherents, ISIL, and other terrorist organizations and criminal networks across the African continent. As the supporting command to CENTCOM for Operation INHERENT RESOLVE, EUCOM continues to provide combat ready forces, force enablers, and critical combat support in the fight against ISIL in both Iraq and Syria. Turkey has expanded its role in the counter-ISIL coalition, allowing the United States to stage armed aircraft from Incirlik Airbase, and has increased its internal security operations against the group. ISIL can no longer view Turkey as a permissive operating environment and will likely attempt targeted attacks against U.S. and Turkish government.

EUCOM's postured forces remain ready for rapid reaction in the volatile environments of North Africa and the Middle East. Special Operations crisis response forces based in Europe continue to provide immediate theater response capability, while remaining prepared to support inter-theater Combatant Command requirements, primarily with aerial lift assets. In 2016, Special Operations Command Europe will assume the role of NATO Response Force Special Operations Component Command. The Marines of the Special Purpose Marine Air Ground Task Force in Spain, Italy, and Romania are ready to respond in Africa and Europe. Strike and associated support aircraft stationed in Germany, Italy, and the United Kingdom are also on alert to react to crises as needed. Strategic facilities and associated access agreements with European Allies and partners enable EUCOM to support this vital mission of protecting U.S. personnel and facilities.

The mature network of U.S. operated bases in the EUCOM AOR provides superb training and power projection facilities in support of steady state operations and contingencies in Europe, Eurasia, Africa, and the Middle East. This footprint is essential to TRANSCOM's global distribution mission and also provides critical basing support for intelligence, surveillance, and reconnaissance assets flying sorties in support of AFRICOM, CENTCOM,

EUCOM, U.S. Special Operations Command, and NATO operations. For example, over the past two years, EUCOM forces provided logistics enabling capabilities at airfields throughout Europe to forces deploying to the Central African Republic, enabling AFRICOM to support the African-led, multinational effort to stabilize that nation. Strategic facilities and associated access agreements with European Allies and partners enable EUCOM to support this vital mission of protecting U.S. personnel and facilities. An increasing number of embassies and consulates, however, remain at risk, on both the African continent and within Europe. AFRICOM maintains no permanent bases outside the Horn of Africa that can support forces assigned to this mission. Moreover, the capabilities available for EUCOM force protection are not keeping pace with the number of at-risk locations and people, and the magnitude of the threats they face.

At the same time, EUCOM is supporting DoD and State Department efforts to establish and/or improve agreements with several eastern European and the Baltic countries. We believe these formal agreements will enhance bilateral relations and also serve as a means to convey the U.S. commitment throughout the region.

Finally, and most importantly, EUCOM plays a supporting role to U.S. North Command and U.S. Pacific Command in defense of the homeland.

IV. **EUCOM Capabilities and Resource Requirements**

Setting the Theater. Given the historic changes in our security environment, we must reassess how our resources meet the most imminent and dangerous threats. EUCOM supports the Department's strategy providing a mixture of assurance to our NATO Allies and Partners and activities that deter Russia. As the dynamics of this strategy continue to shift, EUCOM finds that ERI fills many of the personnel, equipment, and resource gaps we need to meet the Russian aggression. As stated earlier, our current force posture in Europe has been based on Russia as a strategic partner. EUCOM greatly appreciates the authorization and appropriations for ERI by Congress over the past two years, which has mitigated the risks and improved EUCOM's ability to meet its strategy. ERI has also reduced the challenges associated with reductions in our permanent force posture. EUCOM finds itself in a shifted paradigm where the strategic threat presented by Putin's Russia requires we readdress our force allocation processes to provide a credible assurance against what remains the only nation capable of strategic warfare against the homeland. Looking forward we will need to continue to appropriate prioritize the requirements of this theater. EUCOM will most likely require continued Congressional support in the future–

at a minimum of FY17 PB levels –as we effectuate all elements of the planning efforts currently underway. Additional assets are required from Army, Navy and the Air Force to ensure we are able to perform our missions within the AOR. Further, EUCOM needs additional intelligence collection platforms, such as the U2 or the RC 135 to assist the increased collection requirements in the theater.

The augmentation of additional forces and APS in the FY17 budget continue the process of helping EUCOM meet several of its resource needs. The challenge EUCOM faces is ensuring it is able to meet its strategic obligations while primarily relying on rotational forces from the continental United States. Congressional support for ERI helps mitigate this challenge. The European-based U.S. infrastructure that supports EUCOM, CENTCOM, AFRICOM, and SOCOM exists as a result of the established relations between EUCOM forces and host nations. The constant presence of U.S. forces in Europe since World War II has enabled the United States to enjoy the relatively free access we have come to count on—and require—in times of crisis. Further force reductions will likely reduce our access and host-nation permissions to operate from key strategic locations during times of crisis. I am aware, however, of the tremendous demands on our current force structure and the numerous competing factors involved in managing the force.

Combatant Commanders Exercise and Engagement Training and Transformation (CE2T2) Fund. The CE2T2 fund is used to train U.S. Joint Forces at the strategic and operational levels. The CE2T2 has been instrumental to fund the EUCOM Joint Exercise Program, support interoperability with NATO and sustain theater security cooperation through EUCOM regional exercises. The CE2T2 is the only funding the COCOM has that is identified for Joint Training and establishes the foundation of the theater Joint Exercise portfolio. We encourage Congress to continue funding CE2T2. CE2T2 funding increases the readiness of our Joint Force, improves opportunities for our organic, rotational and regional aligned forces to jointly train with and engage with our Allies and Partners.

European Reassurance Initiative (ERI) Requirements. In FY17, we seek to continue a majority of the initiatives previously funded in FY15 and FY16. However, as you have seen, the FY17 ERI request greatly expands our effort to reassure allies and deter Russian aggression.

We plan to continue to pursue the lines of effort currently underway in FY17: (1) increase the level of rotational military presence in Europe; (2) execute additional bilateral and multilateral exercises and training with allies and partners; (3) enhance prepositioning of U.S. equipment in Europe; (4) continue to improve our infrastructure to allow for greater responsiveness; and (5) intensify efforts to build partner capacity with newer NATO members and partners. However, in light of the new security environment, in addition to the continuance of assurance measures, we are strengthening our posture in Europe.

EUCOM Headquarters Manning. Since the end of the Cold War 25 years ago, EUCOM forces and resources have been on a steady decline while our nation appropriately refocused its global security efforts elsewhere. We embarked on a policy of 'hugging the bear' with what we perceived was a former adversary turned strategic partner. The current force structure in Europe, most recently influenced by the 2012 Defense Strategic Guidance and our rebalance to the Asia/Pacific, is roughly 80% smaller than in 1991–making it the smallest COCOM–and is resourced with the strategic assumption that Russia is a partner, not a threat. EUCOM understands Congressional desire to reduce the size of headquarters across the Department. However, Congressional mandates to further reduce headquarter sizes come as the command is transforming from one focused on theater security cooperation to one focused on warfighting.

EUCOM's Footprint Network. As EUCOM continues to implement the 2014 European Infrastructure Consolidation (EIC) decisions, we will ensure that remaining 1 properly supports operational requirements and strategic commitments. The Department is considering whether an emerging need exists to augment the remaining infrastructure to support assurance and deterrence activities in Europe. As discussed earlier, Congressional approval of last year's ERI last year permitted the deployment of an European Activity Set (for training purposes) into theater, while the FY17 request seeks Congressional authorization and appropriation for APS (for crisis response). This equipment in the EUCOM AOR supports the rapid introduction of forces, reduces demands on the transportation system, and appreciably shortens response times. Just as important, it helps assure Allies of continuing U.S. commitment and supports a wide spectrum of options, from traditional crisis response to irregular warfare.

Key Military Construction Projects (MILCON). EUCOM's FY17 military construction program continues to support key posture initiatives, recapitalize infrastructure, and consolidate enduring locations. I appreciate Congress's willingness to continue to fund these priorities, in particular ERI projects, the Landstuhl Regional Medical Center/Rhine Ordnance Barracks theater medical consolidation and recapitalization project (ROBMC), and the relocation of the Joint

Intelligence Operations Center Europe (JIOCEUR) and Joint Analysis Center (JAC) to Croughton, United Kingdom.

ROBMC remains one of the command's highest priority military construction projects, providing a vitally important replacement to theater-based combat and contingency operation medical support from the aged and failing infrastructure at the current facility. This project is vital to continuing the availability of the highest level trauma care for U.S. warfighters injured in the EUCOM, CENTCOM, and AFRICOM theaters.

Another key EUCOM MILCON priority project is the consolidation of the Joint Intelligence Operations Center Europe Analytic Center and other intelligence elements at RAF Croughton, UK. The Department requested Phase 1 planning and design funding for the consolidation during FY15, with three phases of MILCON construction in FY15-17 respectively. Phases 1 and 2 have been authorized and appropriated over the past two legislative cycles. We anticipate the construction completion will occur in FY20/21. The planned replacement facility will consolidate intelligence operations into an efficient, purpose-built building which will save the U.S. Government $74 million per year and reduce significant operational risk associated with the current substandard and deteriorating facilities. The RAF Croughton site also ensures continuation of the strong EUCOM-UK intelligence relationships and our sponsorship of the co-located NATO Intelligence Fusion Center. The maintenance of our intelligence relationships and the intelligence sharing we maintain with the UK and NATO remains vital to EUCOM's capability to conduct military operations from and within Europe.

Information Operations. As mentioned previously, Russia dedicates enormous resources and intelligence efforts in shaping its information operations domain. This is a key enabler for its aggressive hybrid tactics executed in Eastern Europe to distribute its propaganda campaign and help fabricate facts on the ground when needed. EUCOM's efforts in coordination with the interagency on countering this messaging campaign are critical in our overall assurance and deterrence measures.

V.   Conclusion

As I prepare to conclude my time in command, I would like to reiterate how proud I am to have been given the opportunity to Command this team of professionals. EUCOM is a tremendous organization doing extraordinary things with limited resources to ensure we achieve our mission and objectives.

I cannot emphasize enough the somber reality that Europe will remain central to our national security interests. From having fought two world wars in part on European soil to the current instability in the east and south of Europe, our nation must remain indisputably invested in a region that is inexorably tied to our own freedom, security and economic prosperity. The Russia problem set is not going away, and presents a new long term challenge for the EUCOM area of responsibility and our nation. Russia poses an existential threat to the United States, and to the NATO alliance as a whole. It applies an impressive mixture of all elements of national power to pursue its national objectives, to include regular reminders of its nuclear capabilities. While Russia understands the importance of NATO and its Article 5 commitment, it has embarked on a campaign to corrupt and undermine targeted NATO countries through a strategy of indirect, or "hybrid," warfare.

Besides dealing with an aggressive Russia, Europe also faces the challenges of ISIL, managing the flow of migrants, and foreign terrorist fighters from the Levant and Middle East. In my opinion, these new threats emanating from the south and integrating throughout the continent will get worse before they get better. They will continue to stress the already strained European security elements, which will only embolden our common state and non-state adversaries.

EUCOM needs to be better postured to meet our assigned missions, including those in support of AFRICOM, CENTCOM and other combatant commands. With your support of the FY17 budget request, EUCOM will be better postured to meet these assigned missions. Additionally, EUCOM needs Congress' support for a credible and enduring capability that assures, deters, and defends with a coordinated whole-of-government approach. This EUCOM team will continue to relentlessly pursue our mission to reestablish a Europe that is whole, free, at peace, and prosperous.

General Phillip M. Breedlove

Gen. Philip M. Breedlove is Commander, Supreme Allied Command, Europe, SHAPE, Belgium and Headquarters, U.S. European Command, Stuttgart, Germany.

General Breedlove was raised in Forest Park, Ga., and was commissioned in 1977 as a distinguished graduate of Georgia Tech's ROTC program. He has been assigned to numerous operational, command and staff positions, and has completed nine overseas tours, including two remote tours. He has commanded a fighter squadron, an operations group, three fighter wings, and a numbered air force. Additionally, he has served as Vice Chief of Staff of the U.S. Air Force, Washington, D.C. Operations Officer in the Pacific Command Division on the Joint Staff; Executive Officer to the Commander of Headquarters Air Combat Command; the Senior Military Assistant to the Secretary of the Air Force; and Vice Director for Strategic Plans and Policy on the Joint Staff.

Prior to assuming his current position, General Breedlove served as the Commander, U.S. Air Forces in Europe; Commander, U.S. Air Forces Africa; Commander, Air Component Command, Ramstein; and Director, Joint Air Power Competence Centre, Kalkar, Germany. He was responsible for Air Forces activities, conducted through 3rd Air Force, in an area of operations covering more than 19 million square miles. This area included 105 countries in Europe, Africa, Asia and the Middle East, and the Arctic and Atlantic oceans. As Vice Chief, he presided over the Air Staff and served as a member of the Joint Chiefs of Staff Requirements Oversight Council and Deputy Advisory Working Group. He assisted the Chief of Staff with organizing, training, and equipping of 680,000 active-duty, Guard, Reserve and civilian forces serving in the United States and overseas. General Breedlove has flown combat missions in Operation Joint Forge/Joint Guardian. He is a command pilot with 3,500 flying hours, primarily in the F-16.

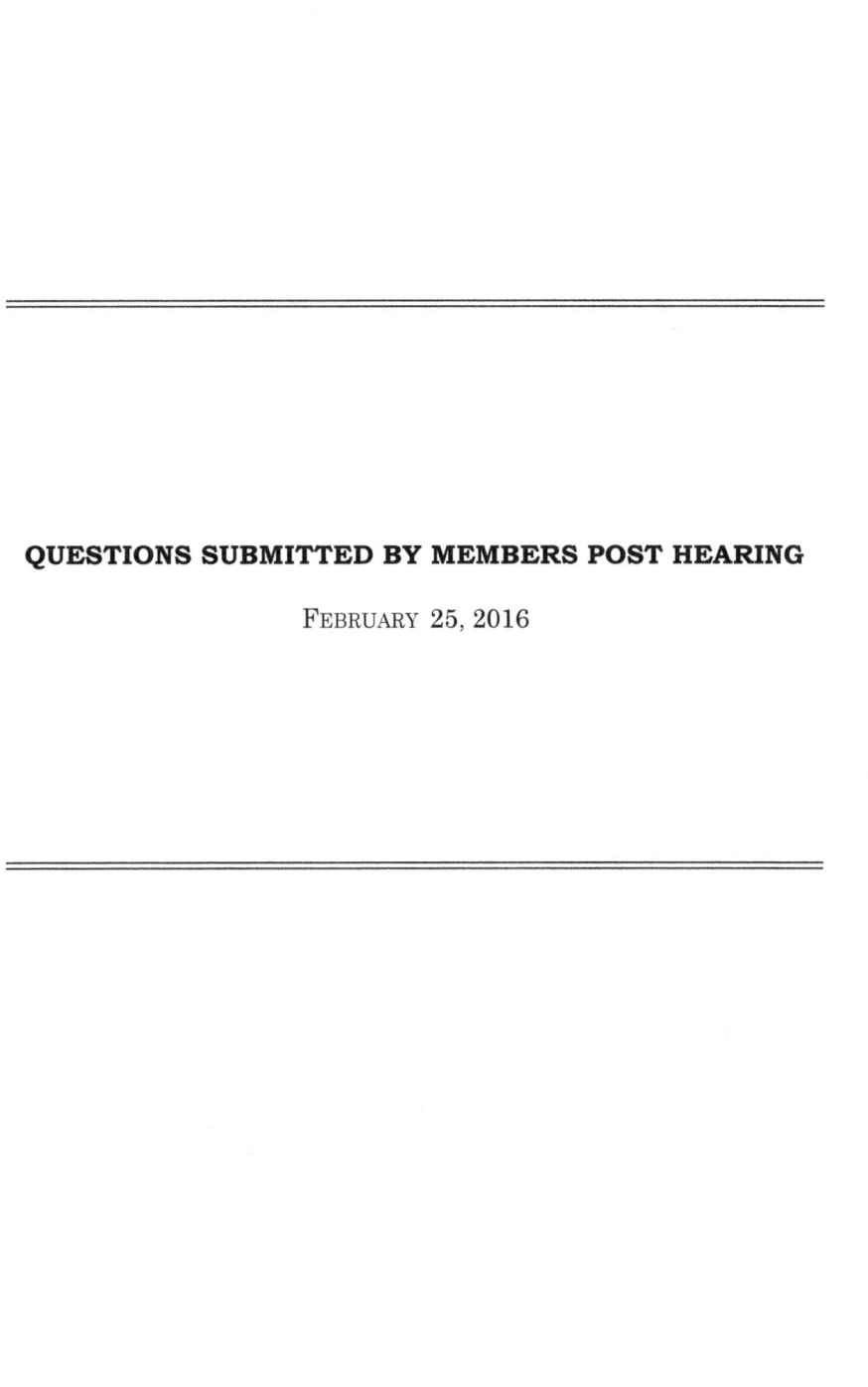

QUESTIONS SUBMITTED BY MEMBERS POST HEARING

FEBRUARY 25, 2016

QUESTION SUBMITTED BY MR. SHUSTER

Mr. SHUSTER. Do you believe we have enough Patriot battalions to support the continued mission of deterrence against Russia?

General BREEDLOVE. [The information referred to is classified and retained in the committee files.]

QUESTION SUBMITTED BY MR. CONAWAY

Mr. CONAWAY. Russia has greatly expanded its distribution of natural gas throughout Europe. This pattern appears to be part of a larger geo-political agenda in countries such as Syria and Ukraine, as witnessed by incursions into Crimea and elsewhere. Natural gas exportation significantly enhances Russia's ability to operate abroad, playing a significant component in an otherwise weakening economy. In view of increased use of Russian natural gas at regional energy facilities that supply heating to numerous U.S. military installations throughout Western Europe, is the expansion of Russian energy not a considerable risk factor?

General BREEDLOVE. Using natural gas from countries who rely on Russian supplies does pose a risk. While not ideal, the United States government is working with our European Allies and partners to determine ways to diversify their energy sources.

QUESTION SUBMITTED BY MR. CASTRO

Mr. CASTRO. Has NATO discussed changes to Article 6 to include non-conventional attacks such as a cyber attack?

General BREEDLOVE. Article 6 of the Washington Treaty relates generally to the location of an armed attack on a NATO member that could trigger the collective defense provisions of Article 5. While there have been many discussions relating to cyber attacks and Article 5, we are unaware of any specific discussions on Article 6 changes.

It is NATO's articulated policy, expressed in paragraph 72 of the Wales Action Plan (Sep. 5, 2014), that "cyber defense is part of NATO's core task of collective defense." In general, NATO assets exist to protect NATO networks, and allies must protect their own national assets. As set forth in the "Active Engagement, Modern Defence" statement at NATO's Lisbon Summit in November 2010, cyber attacks "can reach a threshold that threatens national and Euro-Atlantic prosperity, security and stability." As NATO Secretary General Rasmussen said in October 2010, there is a "constructive ambiguity" with regard to the use of Article 5 of the Washington Treaty, including in the case of cyber attacks. Such a decision would be taken by the North Atlantic Council on a case-by-case basis.

QUESTION SUBMITTED BY MR. HUNTER

Mr. HUNTER. Russia has greatly expanded its distribution of natural gas throughout Europe. This pattern appears to be part of a larger geo-political agenda in countries such as Syria and Ukraine, as witnessed by incursions into Crimea and elsewhere. Natural gas exportation significantly enhances Russia's ability to operate abroad, playing a significant component in an otherwise weakening economy. In view of increased use of Russian natural gas at regional energy facilities that supply heating to numerous U.S. military installations throughout Western Europe, is the expansion of Russian energy not a considerable risk factor? The Army is about to construct a major new medical center at the Rhine Ordnance Barracks Installation in Germany, a facility to replace Landstuhl Regional Medical Center. This facility provides medical care for service personnel and their families in the European Theater from each branch of the military. There remains a possibility that Russian natural gas will be the exclusive energy source for heat at the facility. Would such an acquisition policy be counter-productive to NATO's efforts to address Russia's recent posturing?

General BREEDLOVE. No, we do not believe this acquisition policy is currently counter-productive to NATO's efforts. We recognize that in the long term overreliance on Russian natural gas could prove problematic. The United States government is working with our NATO Allies and partners on energy diversification efforts.

_____

QUESTIONS SUBMITTED BY MR. GIBSON

Mr. GIBSON. What is your assessment of the criticality of the Global Response Force? Also, what is your assessment of the level of risk of continuing the Army drawdown, and what it would mean in terms of buying down risk to station an Armored Brigade Combat Team and a Combat Aviation Brigade in Europe?

General BREEDLOVE. [The information referred to is classified and retained in the committee files.]

_____

QUESTIONS SUBMITTED BY MR. SCOTT

Mr. SCOTT. Can you describe the infrastructure and capabilities European Command (EUCOM) needs now in order achieve information and cyber dominance in a hybrid conflict?

General BREEDLOVE. A future conflict will be characterized by a combination of regular, irregular, and cyberspace-based warfare typically supported by an aggressive propaganda campaign. In order to achieve information dominance in such a conflict in its area of operations, EUCOM would need to be able to inform, persuade and influence both foreign decision makers and population groups. Specifically, it would require both the capacity and capabilities to conduct sustained "influence operations." While EUCOM has some capacity and capability to conduct these kinds of "influence operations," shortfalls exist that create risk to U.S. objectives in a hybrid conflict. Capacity could be achieved through an increase in the numbers of qualified analysts available to the command, both in reach back and at the headquarters, sub-unified command level (Special Operations Command Europe), and the component level (Army, Air Force, Navy, Marines). It is key to have qualified persons who can conduct the activities that lead to dominance, including Military Information Support Operations. We require new influence operations capabilities emphasizing research, analysis, and assessment, as well as the employment of social media. The capacity and capabilities we need are very difficult, if not impossible, to "surge." Russia, as we know, is employing many resources in its influence operations in Eastern Europe. Accordingly, EUCOM believes that funding for influence operations should be increased and included in the Department's base budget.

Mr. SCOTT. What are the current gaps in your intelligence, surveillance, and reconnaissance (ISR) capabilities with regard to your combatant command? How does the Joint Surveillance and Target Attack Radar System platform integrate into your current ISR network?

General BREEDLOVE. [The information referred to is classified and retained in the committee files.]

_____

QUESTION SUBMITTED BY MR. TAKAI

Mr. TAKAI. You focused the majority of your testimony on explaining how Russia is our greatest threat. Though most focused on Europe and the Middle East, Russia is also engaged politically and militarily in the Indo-Asia-Pacific. Ships and submarines of the Russian Pacific Fleet and long range aircraft routinely demonstrate Russia's message that it is a Pacific power. America's future demands greater attention to the Asia-Pacific region. Russian ballistic missile and attack submarines remain especially active in the Asia-Pacific. The arrival in late 2015 of Russia's newest class of nuclear ballistic missile submarine (DOLGORUKIY SSBN) in the Far East is part of a modernization program for the Russian Pacific Fleet and signals the seriousness with which Moscow views this region. Your testimony highlighted the importance of maintaining relationships. I quote, "You can't surge trust." The same could be said for relationships with our allies in the Asia-Pacific; the risks associated with major combat operations in the Asia-Pacific theater place a premium on preexisting command relationships.

Don't you think the European Reassurance Initiative could do with less so that resources could be adequately distributed to the growing threat of Russia, and China, and North Korea, in the Asia-Pacific region?

General BREEDLOVE. The European Reassurance Initiative (ERI) is necessary to address the Russian threat to NATO Allies and other partners within the USEUCOM Area of Responsibility (AOR). With the FY17 ERI budget request, we are consciously beginning to address the requirement to take prudent actions now (e.g., store prepositioned Army equipment, provide full-time Armored Brigade Combat Team (ABCT) presence, enhance exercises with Allies, etc.) that will aid in deterring future Russian aggression in Europe. I believe the scope of FY17 ERI is appropriate and necessary to meet the threat in Eruope, and it does not address the challenges in other theaters. However, I am also sensitive to the needs to address emerging requirements in other Combatant Command AORs as well given overall budget constraints.